Beyond Anger and Violence

Other Publications by Stephanie S. Covington

- *Leaving the Enchanted Forest: The Path from Relationship Addiction to Intimacy* (with Liana Beckett)
- *A Woman's Way through The Twelve Steps*
- *A Woman's Way through The Twelve Steps Workbook*
- *A Woman's Way through The Twelve Steps* (Facilitator Guide and DVD)
- *La mujer y su práctica de los Doce Pasos*
- *La mujer y su práctica de los Doce Pasos: Libro de ejercicios*
- *Awakening Your Sexuality: A Guide for Recovering Women*
- *Women in Recovery: Understanding Addiction*
- *Mujeres en recuperación: Entendiendo la adicción*
- *Beyond Trauma: A Healing Journey for Women* (Facilitator Guide, A Workbook for Women, and DVDs)
- *Healing Trauma: Strategies for Abused Women* (CD-ROM)
- *Voices: A Program of Self-Discovery and Empowerment for Girls* (Facilitator Guide and Interactive Journal)
- *Women and Addiction: A Gender-Responsive Approach* (Manual and DVD)
- *Helping Women Recover: A Program for Treating Addiction* (Facilitator Guide and A Woman's Journal)
- *Helping Women Recover: A Program for Treating Addiction: Special Edition for Use in the Criminal Justice System* (Facilitator Guide and A Woman's Journal)
- *Helping Men Recover: A Program for Treating Addiction* (with Dan Griffin and Rick Dauer) (Facilitator Guide and A Man's Workbook)
- *Helping Men Recover: A Program for Treating Addiction: Special Edition for Use in the Criminal Justice System* (with Dan Griffin and Rick Dauer) (Facilitator Guide and A Man's Workbook)
- *Beyond Violence: A Prevention Program for Criminal Justice–Involved Women* (Facilitator Guide, Participant Workbook, and DVD)

Beyond Anger and Violence

A PROGRAM FOR WOMEN

Stephanie S. Covington

WILEY

CONTENTS

INTRODUCTION

We see the effects of anger and violence all around us, in the news, in television shows and motion pictures, and often in our families and relationships. Even though anger is the most common emotion, many people find it difficult to understand and to regulate their anger. *Beyond Anger and Violence* is a program for women who struggle with issues related to anger.

Some women feel a lot of anger. They may fear that their anger will get out of control. Some women have felt rage and have been aggressive or abusive toward others they care about, including children. Some women seethe in silence and don't feel good about the way they handle anger. Some women turn their anger inward. They may become depressed. They may harm themselves by cutting or burning themselves. Some women are seldom aware of feeling anger until they drink or use drugs; then they may explode. Some women have learned that anger allows them to intimidate others, get attention, or obtain what they want, so their anger becomes a tool they can use to push others away. For some women, anger has become a survival tool; it has helped them to survive their families, relationships, schools, and/or their neighborhoods.

Other women have borne the brunt of another person's anger. They may be victims of abuse or violence in a relationship. Their anger is often complex because it is intertwined with hurt. Women who have experienced abuse may have been told that they should "just get over it" because they can't do anything about the past or because "it was a long time ago."

This Program

Beyond Anger and Violence: A Program for Women, is not a traditional anger management program. It is designed to explain and explore the topic of anger on multiple levels: the personal level (the anger you feel); the relationship level, including anger directed toward you; and the effects of anger and violence in our communities and society at large. Because women who struggle with anger often have difficulty with relationships, the program is also designed to help you develop social skills by means of a group process.

Beyond Anger and Violence is designed to help you identify the sources of your anger, how you deal with that anger, and anger's effects in your life. You can learn to develop ways of managing your anger that are empowering and do not cause you problems. The program is structured to work on two levels: one is the anger that you experience, in whatever form; the other is the anger and violence you have experienced from others. Experiencing another's anger and violence often creates trauma, so *Beyond Anger and Violence* explores the role of trauma and posttraumatic stress in women's lives. The holistic approach to dealing with anger in this program is designed to facilitate healing. You will also have an opportunity to learn and practice new behaviors that can lead to a more peaceful life.

Orientation Session

Overview of the Program

Beyond Anger and Violence: A Program for Women, is divided into four parts: Self, Relationships, Community, and Society. These four content areas will guide you in understanding important issues relating to anger and violence in the lives of many women, both inside and outside your program group.

During this program, you will attend this orientation session and twenty additional sessions with the members of your group. With them, you will have new experiences and learn new ways of looking at the world. The facilitator who will conduct the sessions has experience in working with women who have reacted with anger and/or force toward others, and she understands the issues.

Taking part in this group will allow you to explore how seeing and experiencing anger and violence in your life has affected you and the decisions you have made. You will find support from the other women. As you explore important issues together, you will learn new ways to cope and better ways to make decisions. You will experience a greater sense of power, inner strength, and peace.

The *Beyond Anger and Violence* program aims

- To provide a place where you can reflect and learn more about yourself;

- To provide information so you can better understand the relationships among your thoughts, feelings, and behaviors;

- To help you understand the effects of your family, your relationships, your community, and the larger society on your life;

- To help you understand more about the roles of anger and violence in your life;

- To provide an opportunity for you to learn new skills, including skills in communication, conflict resolution, decision making, and calming or self-soothing techniques; and

- To help you become part of a group of women working to create a less violent world.

Your Workbook

This workbook is a place for you to record your experiences during the journey that you are about to begin in the *Beyond Anger and Violence* program. Using this workbook will help you to remember what you learn, think, and feel. The workbook contains

- Some of the activities you will do during the group sessions,

- Summaries of information that you will receive in the group sessions, and

- Activities for you to do after each session.

The activities will help you to examine many parts of your life. There are no right or wrong answers, and your responses will not be checked. You may be asked to share some of your responses in the group sessions, but this is voluntary, and other group members will be sharing as well. You do not need to worry about your handwriting or spelling. This workbook is a tool to help you with your own growth and recovery.

You will keep your workbook to use between sessions. It is your responsibility to remember to bring your workbook to each group session.

Group Introductions

The following activity asks you for information you can use to introduce yourself to the group. This introduction allows you and the other group members to begin to get to know one another.

1. My name: _____
   _____

2. When and where I was born: _____
   _____

3. How I identify myself (including culture, ethnicity, race): _____
   _____
   _____

4. The people in my family (may include a husband or live-in partner, children, mother, father, brothers, sisters, or whomever you consider your immediate family): _____
   _____
   _____
   _____
   _____

5. One thing I like about myself or a special gift that I have: _____
   _____
   _____

Topics Covered in This Program

1. The ways in which our thoughts and feelings affect our behaviors

2. Ways to better manage our feelings, especially the powerful and painful ones

3. The impacts of families and relationships on our lives

4. Information about abusive and healthy relationships

5. The role of anger in women's lives

6. The effects of our communities on our lives, including support for violence in our communities

7. Ways to make amends and restitution

8. The value of envisioning a more peaceful world

Group Agreements

Your facilitator has explained the purpose of group agreements. They describe behaviors that will help your group to be a safe, respectful, and supportive space for each group member. Please use the spaces below to record the agreements made by your group.

Our Group Agreements

There are three agreements that are important for any group:

1. *Confidentiality.* Group members need to honor one another's confidentiality. What is said in this room stays in this room. No personal information revealed in this room may be repeated outside this room.

2. *Sobriety.* No one may attend a group session while under the influence of alcohol or another drug.

3. *Safety.* There will be no physical or emotional abuse. Part of safety is showing respect for one another and for the uniqueness of every person's thoughts, feelings, experiences, and responses. Respect is essential. We will let people express themselves in their own ways. Being rude or abusive to another group member is *not* okay.

Here are some examples of other typical group agreements:

4. *Timing.* Our sessions will start on time and end on time.

5. *Attendance.* Regular group attendance is important. We all agree to show up at all the sessions.

6. *Eating or drinking.* There will be no eating or drinking during the group sessions (except perhaps for bottled water).

7. *Sharing.* Everyone in the group should have the time to contribute and share the experience. We will try to let everyone have a chance to talk. We will not interrupt other group members but will let them finish before we respond or add something.

8. *Participation.* We will try to assist one another in feeling safe enough to share and participate. We will ask questions to help us learn and grow. However, everyone is entitled to "pass" when asked a question or when asked to do an activity that requires participation.

9. *Socialization.* Contact with other group members outside the regular group session is permitted.

Triggers and Coping Tools

A *trigger* is a reminder of a traumatic event. It can be something you see, hear, smell, or feel. It can be a person, a place, or anything that reminds you of a traumatic event. It is important to have grounding or coping tools to help us stay in the present. Here are two coping tools you used in the group.

Five Senses

This is an exercise you can do to relax or calm yourself and to bring yourself into the present moment.

1. Close your eyes or lower your eyelids.

2. Relax for a few moments. Take a few deep breaths and exhale slowly.

3. Open your eyes when you are ready.

4. Silently, identify five things you can see around you.

5. Now identify four things you could feel or touch.

6. Identify three things you can hear.

7. Identify two things you can smell.

8. Finally, identify what you can taste right now.

Breathing and Exhaling

This is another good exercise to do to relax or calm yourself.

1. Stand up.

2. Set your feet a little distance apart so that you feel stable. Take a few deep breaths.

3. Relax your shoulders and just drop your hands to your sides. Let your arms and hands just dangle, relaxed. Relax your shoulders and arms.

Beyond Anger and Violence: A Program for Women

4. Take in a long, deep breath through your nose and blow it out through your mouth like a big gust of wind.

5. Inhale again, and then again let the air out by blowing it out of your mouth.

6. Remember to relax your shoulders and arms.

7. Do the inhaling and exhaling three more times.

Statistics on Violence in the United States

1. Children born into poverty have such a high risk of exposure to violence that they are almost certain to be affected by trauma (*Women's Law Project, 2002*).

2. More than thirty million children in the United States live in low-income families, and fourteen million children live in poverty (*Wight, Chau, & Aratani, 2010*).

3. Violence is more prevalent in children's television programming than in other types of programming (*Wilson, 2002*).

4. The average child who watches two hours of cartoons a day will see nearly 10,000 violent acts a year (*Center for Communication and Social Policy, 1998*).

5. Three million to ten million children are exposed to or witness domestic violence each year (*Family Violence Prevention Fund, 2009*).

6. In homes where domestic violence occurs, children are seriously abused or neglected at a rate that is 1,500 percent higher than the national average for the general population (*Children's Defense Fund Ohio, 2009*).

7. At least 50 percent of child abuse and neglect cases are associated with alcohol or drug abuse by parents (*Every Child Matters Education Fund, 2008*).

8. Children from violent homes have a higher tendency than other children to commit suicide, abuse drugs or alcohol, and commit violence against their own partners or children (*Whitfield, Anda, Dube, & Felitti, 2003*).

9. One in five girls and one in ten boys are sexually victimized before adulthood (*National Center for Missing and Exploited Children, 2008*).

10. Eighty-five percent of the victims of intimate partner violence are women (*Catalano, 2012*).

11. One in four women has been the victim of severe physical violence by an intimate partner (*Black et al., 2011*).

12. In the United States in 2010, a woman experienced rape or physical violence by an intimate partner approximately every eleven seconds (*Black et al., 2011*).

13. Nearly one in five women has been raped (*Black et al., 2011*).

14. Women experience two million injuries from intimate partner violence each year (*Centers for Disease Control and Prevention, 2008*).

The chart below compares the homicide rate in the United States with that of other countries.

International Homicide Rates
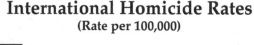

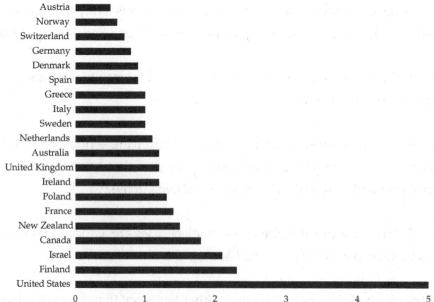

Source: Global Study on Homicide 2011: Trends, Context, Data, by United Nations Office on Drugs and Crime, 2011, Vienna: United Nations Office on Drugs and Crime. Retrieved from http://www.unodc.org/documents/data-and-analysis/statistics/Homicide/Globa_study_on_homicide_2011_web.pdf

Definition of Violence

Violence is "the intentional use of physical force or power—threatened or actual—against oneself, another person, or a group or community, that either results in or has a high likelihood of resulting in injury, death, psychological harm, inhibited development, or deprivation" (*World Health Organization, 2004*). In this definition, violence is divided into three types, based on how it happens:

- *Self-directed violence* (the perpetrator and the victim are the same person) includes self-harm and suicide.

- *Interpersonal violence* (between individuals) includes family and intimate-partner violence and community violence.

- *Collective violence* (committed by larger groups) includes social, political, and economic violence. Examples are war and genocide.

In each of these categories, violence can be inflicted in four ways: by physical, sexual, or psychological attack or by deprivation.

Here are some more definitions that help to explain the differences between abusive behaviors that can happen in a relationship. *Use of force* is an overall term that refers to physically, verbally, or emotionally damaging behaviors used by one person toward another in order to gain short-term control of relationship dynamics. *Violence* refers to any force used with the intention of causing injury. *Abuse* refers to isolated and random acts of violence. *Battering* is a systematic pattern of violence, the threat of violence, and/or coercively controlling behaviors, used with the intention of exerting power, creating fear, and/or controlling the other person in a relationship over the long term. Coercive control is the cornerstone of battering, so battering does not need to include physical violence in order to be harmful.

The Social-Ecological Model (People in the Environment)

To try to understand violence, we need to look at the factors that put people at risk for experiencing or perpetrating violence. The *Beyond Anger and Violence* program is based on a social-ecological model. This means that there is no one thing that explains why violence occurs. The model considers the complex interrelationships between individuals, their interpersonal relationships, their communities, and societal factors. This includes cultural factors.

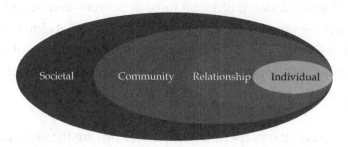

Source: "Violence—A Global Health Problem," by L. L. Dahlberg and E. G. Krug, 2002, in E. G. Krug, L. L. Dahlberg, J. A. Mercy, A. B. Zwi, and R. Lorenzo (Eds.), *World Report on Violence and Health* (pp. 1–56), Geneva: World Health Organization. Also see Centers for Disease Control and Prevention, *The Social-Ecological Model: A Framework for Prevention*, retrieved from http://www.cdc.gov/ violenceprevention/overview/social-ecologicalmodel.html

The first layer, Individual, is a person's biological history (for example, any mental health and substance abuse patterns in her family) and her personal history (for example, her life experiences and important events). It is important to think about how these influences increase a woman's chance of becoming a victim of violence and also increase her chance of committing violence against (victimizing) another person.

The second layer, Relationship, is a woman's relationships with friends, family members, and intimate partners. Some of these may increase a woman's risk of becoming a victim of violence or committing violence against another person.

The third layer, Community, is where a woman lives and works (the neighborhood, schools, workplaces, and available services) and how these places and the relationships within them affect her likelihood of becoming a victim of violence or of committing violence.

The fourth layer, Societal, is the society a woman lives in. It includes social and cultural norms (things that are common in our society), such as whether the environment encourages or discourages violence. Economic, educational, and class factors also are in this layer.

For each of these levels, the risk factors for being abused are the same as the risk factors for being an abuser.

Individual

1. The risk of having mental health issues greatly increases if a person has experienced multiple traumatic events in childhood (*Messina & Grella, 2006*).

Beyond Anger and Violence: A Program for Women

2. Living in a family with multiple problems (such as violence, drug and alcohol abuse, and neglect) increases a child's chance of gang involvement (*Office of Juvenile Justice and Delinquency Prevention, 2008*).

3. Women who have experienced deprivation and dysfunctional or violent relationships in early life often have high levels of physical and mental health problems (*Felitti & Anda, 2010*).

4. Using alcohol and other drugs is a way of coping with feelings of hopelessness and despair. Many women who are arrested are substance abusers (*Covington, 2007*).

Relationship

1. Women who are victims of childhood abuse are more likely to react violently than women who are not (*Pollock, Mullings, & Crouch, 2006*).

2. Women often have their first encounters with the law as juveniles who have run away from home in order to escape violence and physical or sexual abuse (*Covington, 2003*).

3. More than one in three women (over 35 percent) in the United States have experienced rape, physical violence, and/or stalking by an intimate partner (*Black et al., 2011*).

4. In 2010, an estimated 926,000 women experienced intimate partner violence. Most of these women had been previously victimized by the same intimate partner (*Catalano, 2012*).

5. Women who are violated or abused by people with whom they are in relationships—people whom they trust—often turn to alcohol or drugs as a way to numb the pain of being betrayed (*Covington & Surrey, 2000*).

Community

1. Sixty-one percent of people in the United States think that crimes (such as muggings, shootings, rapes, and burglaries) have increased in their communities in the past five years (*Federal Bureau of Investigation, 2008*).

2. Violent crime rates are highest in economically challenged communities (*Pollock, Mullings, & Crouch, 2006*).

3. The U.S. Department of Justice estimates that one in five women experiences rape or attempted rape during her college years, and that less than 5 percent of such rapes are reported (*Taylor & Gaskin-Laniyan, 2007*).

Society

1. African American and Native American women experience domestic violence more often than white women do (*National Organization for Women, 2009*).

2. A person can be traumatized by witnessing violence as well as by suffering it. Trauma can also result from the stigmatization that comes from poverty, incarceration, sexual orientation, and being of a minority race (*Covington, 2007*).

3. Women often suppress the anger they feel from experiencing economic and social inequality (*Walley-Jean, 2009*).

4. Historical or cultural trauma happens to groups of people who lose their culture. In the United States, these groups include African Americans, Native Americans, Native Hawaiians, and the Japanese families who were put in internment camps during World War II (*Duran, Firehammer, & Gonzalez, 2008*).

All these statistics can be overwhelming. That is a normal reaction to this information. However, it is important to acknowledge the violence in our world. A quotation from Helen Keller may help in getting a sense of balance about these things.

Although the world is full of suffering, it is also full of the overcoming of it.
—*Helen Keller*

Creating a Container

Talking about violence and hearing other women's stories can be emotionally overwhelming. In the past, the feelings these things generated may have caused you to use alcohol or drugs, to shut down, or to become angry. In this program, you will learn different ways of dealing with these feelings. One way is to visualize a container that you can temporarily put some of your feelings and concerns into when you need to focus on something else. As you become more comfortable doing this during the program, you will discover that it is a quick and effective way to temporarily reduce your stress and anxiety.

1. Think about your experience. Are there any thoughts or feelings that came up that were difficult for you?

2. Close your eyes or lower your eyelids. Take a deep breath and let it out.

3. Imagine a container of some kind that can hold thoughts and feelings. It might be a trash can, a box with a lock, or even a hole in the ground. Make sure that it has a lid.

4. Now imagine depositing any of those negative or difficult thoughts and feelings into the container. Place all of them in the container, knowing that it's just for a brief period of time. Put the lid on.

5. You can retrieve these items any time you want or need to deal with them. For now, however, you can focus on other things.

6. When you are ready, slowly open your eyes.

Draw your container here.

Discovering Your Anger Style

Read each statement that follows and then circle the number that indicates how much you agree or disagree with the statement. There are no right or wrong answers. Some women are aware of their anger, and some women are not. Discovering your anger style or gaining deeper insight into your anger style can help you to develop healthier ways of recognizing and expressing your anger in your daily life.

1. I believe that physical force is needed to get through to some people.

1	2	3	4	5
Strongly Disagree	Disagree	Not Sure	Agree	Strongly Agree

2. If I hit someone and hurt the person, he or she was asking for it.

1	2	3	4	5
Strongly Disagree	Disagree	Not Sure	Agree	Strongly Agree

3. I am most likely to get physical with someone when I feel that he or she was trying to make me look bad.

1	2	3	4	5
Strongly Disagree	Disagree	Not Sure	Agree	Strongly Agree

4. In an argument, I would feel more annoyed with myself if I cried than if I hit the other person.

1	2	3	4	5
Strongly Disagree	Disagree	Not Sure	Agree	Strongly Agree

5. The best thing about physical force is that it makes the other person get in line.

1	2	3	4	5
Strongly Disagree	Disagree	Not Sure	Agree	Strongly Agree

6. If someone challenged me to a fight in public, I'd feel like a coward if I backed down.

1	2	3	4	5
Strongly Disagree	Disagree	Not Sure	Agree	Strongly Agree

7. After I lash out physically at someone, I would like to make sure the person never annoys me again.

1	2	3	4	5
Strongly Disagree	Disagree	Not Sure	Agree	Strongly Agree

8. I am more likely to lash out physically when someone shows me up in public.

1	2	3	4	5
Strongly Disagree	Disagree	Not Sure	Agree	Strongly Agree

(Continued)

9. During a physical fight, I feel out of control.

1	2	3	4	5
Strongly Disagree	Disagree	Not Sure	Agree	Strongly Agree

10. I am most likely to get physical when I've been under a lot of stress and some little thing pushes me over the edge.

1	2	3	4	5
Strongly Disagree	Disagree	Not Sure	Agree	Strongly Agree

11. After a physical fight, I feel drained and guilty.

1	2	3	4	5
Strongly Disagree	Disagree	Not Sure	Agree	Strongly Agree

12. After I lash out physically at someone, I would like the person to recognize how upset he or she made me and how unhappy I was.

1	2	3	4	5
Strongly Disagree	Disagree	Not Sure	Agree	Strongly Agree

13. I believe that my aggression comes from losing my self-control.

1	2	3	4	5
Strongly Disagree	Disagree	Not Sure	Agree	Strongly Agree

14. I am more likely to lash out physically at someone who is annoying me when I am alone with him or her.

1	2	3	4	5
Strongly Disagree	Disagree	Not Sure	Agree	Strongly Agree

15. When I get to the point of physical force, the thing I am most aware of is how upset and shaky I feel.

1	2	3	4	5
Strongly Disagree	Disagree	Not Sure	Agree	Strongly Agree

16. In a heated argument, I am most afraid of saying something terrible that I can never take back.

1	2	3	4	5
Strongly Disagree	Disagree	Not Sure	Agree	Strongly Agree

Now look at your answers. Statements 1 through 8 relate to a style of anger called *anger reactive*. This type of anger is usually about establishing and maintaining a sense of control over other people. Statements 9 through 16 are related to a style of anger called *anger avoidant*. This type of anger is usually about storing or "stuffing" anger (a form of self-control) until it reaches an explosion point. In reviewing your responses, see if you agreed more with the anger-reactive statements or the anger-avoidant statements.

Assignment

Practice putting any uncomfortable feelings into your container and putting a lid on it, in your imagination. Do this before the next group session, and then write or draw about this experience on this page.

Self-Soothing Activity: Palms Down, Palms Up

Anytime you need to let go of something negative and receive the positive, you can take a few minutes to do this activity.

1. Sit comfortably with your back straight. Close your eyes or lower your eyelids and focus on your breathing. Take a slow, deep breath while counting to four. Then exhale slowly, counting to four.

2. Do this four more times until your breathing is slow and relaxed.

3. Keep breathing slowly and evenly. Hold your hands gently in front of you with your palms up and imagine them holding all the negative or upsetting thoughts and feelings you have had today.

4. Now turn your palms down. Imagine yourself emptying your hands of all the negative or upsetting things you've been carrying today. Let go of them.

5. Keep breathing slowly. Now turn your palms up. Your palms are up and open to receive positive energy, positive thoughts and feelings. Your palms are open to receive support and help.

6. Now slowly open your eyes.

PART A

Self

Thinking Our Thoughts

In this program, you will explore four different levels of your life, starting with the individual level, the self. Your risk for becoming a victim or victimizer (perpetrator of violence) is influenced by your personal history, including your family background, level of education, race, socioeconomic status, how you behave, and how others behave toward you. Things that contribute to risk are being abused in childhood or adulthood, mental health issues, alcohol and substance abuse, and a history of behaving aggressively (*World Health Organization, 2004*).

In Part A, you will be examining how your individual thoughts and feelings influence your behaviors. This will provide you with an opportunity to get to know yourself better.

The goals for Session One are
- To examine typical habits in thinking, and
- To understand how our thoughts influence our feelings and behaviors.

The Spiral of Violence and Nonviolence

This spiral illustrates violence and nonviolence. The downward part on the left is the spiral of violence. The line in the middle represents aggression, violence, or use of force. As anger and aggression (which can lead to violence) become more a part of your life, they constrict and limit your life. For victims, this may mean being shut off from contact with family members, friends, and social services—feeling isolated and alone. A victim also may be afraid to go to places and people that can help. For victimizers (perpetrators), this may mean trying to keep the aggression and violence a secret and hiding from law enforcement agencies. For both, the inner self (thoughts, feelings, and values) becomes more limited and hidden, and the outer self (behavior and relationships) becomes more isolated.

The upward part of the spiral on the right is the spiral of nonviolence. The center line still represents violence, because if you have experienced violence, even if you are in the process of recovery or healing, the experience of violence does not go away. However, in the upward spiral, there is increasing room for growth and healing and many other life experiences. As you stop participating in aggressive or violent behavior and you begin to heal from the violence, the possibility of experiencing meaningful change in your life is created. The goal is to become whole: to have your inner self connected to your outer self. Then there can be truth and integrity in your life.

Spiral of Violence and Nonviolence

(Transformation)

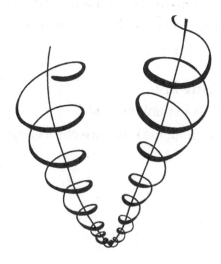

Violence
(Constriction)

Nonviolence
(Expansion)

Cognitive Distortion

When your mind convinces you of something that isn't really true, it is called a *cognitive distortion*. Such thoughts also are called *thinking errors*, *negative self-talk*, *twisted thinking*, and *distorted information processing*. Such distortions or inaccurate thoughts are usually used to reinforce negative thinking or emotions. Here are some examples of this type of thinking:

- *Overgeneralizing*. You tend to speak in terms of something "always" or "never" happening. For example, if you fail to do something, you may say, "I never remember things I'm supposed to." You may also interpret events this way and say things like, "Why does this stuff always happen to me?"

- *All-or-nothing thinking*. Things are either right or wrong, black or white, great or horrible. There are only either/or categories; there is no middle ground or gray area. For example, if something doesn't live up to your expectations in some area, you may see it as a total failure.

- *Mental filtering*. You may let one fact or situation or event color your view of things so that you see everything through a darkened lens. For example, if you have been abused by a male, you may think that all men are rotten or dangerous.

- *Disqualifying the positive*. You may ignore or explain away any positive facts or experiences. If you can rationalize that something good "doesn't count" for some reason, you can maintain a negative belief system.

- *Personalizing*. You may take responsibility or blame for something bad that you had no control over. You may tell yourself, "It must be my fault somehow."

- *Mind reading*. You may decide that someone doesn't like you or thinks she is better than you without getting to know the person or without checking your assumptions if you do know her. When you interpret someone's facial expressions or nonverbal communication with no other input than your own thoughts, you are projecting what is in your mind, not in the other person's.

- *Magnifying or minimizing*. You may give something more credit or more importance than it deserves or you may do the opposite and give it less credit or less importance than is actually called for. Sometimes this is called "making a mountain out of a molehill" or the reverse.

- *Jumping to conclusions.* You may decide early on that something is bad or will turn out badly, even without evidence to support that belief. You may make assumptions about things without waiting for more information. For example, if something is missing, you may assume that a particular person has stolen it before you have searched thoroughly for it.

- *Fortune-telling.* When you assume that you know how things will turn out before they happen, you are fortune-telling. If you are looking at things through a darkened lens, you probably will predict a doom-and-gloom scenario.

- *Emotional reasoning.* You may let your feelings direct your interpretation of things. For example, if you are feeling "down," you may interpret things people do or say in a negative way. If you are feeling "up," you may see things through "rose-colored glasses." In short, you assume, "I feel it, therefore it must be true."

- *Using "should" and "must" statements.* Your expectations may be directed by a rigid list of rules you have about how you and others should behave. If you think that you "should" or "should not" be a certain way, you may feel guilt when you don't think you live up to that expectation. Similarly, you may frequently be disappointed when others do not live up to the rules. If you use "should," "must," and "ought" often in your thinking or conversation, you may be setting yourself up for feelings of anger, frustration, and resentment.

- *Labeling and mislabeling.* This is a mental and verbal way of doing the types of thinking described here. Instead of seeing a person or a behavior or an event as it is, you give it a label that allows you to dismiss or degrade it, in order to reinforce your negative outlook or interpretation. For example, if a person makes a mistake, you may label that person as "stupid."

What are the three types of cognitive distortion that you have used most often?

My Typical Distorted Thinking

When we have thoughts about a situation, we usually have feelings about it too. Both thoughts and feelings affect our behaviors. This table shows some examples.

Situation *What happened?*	Thoughts *What did you think?*	Feelings *How did you feel?*	Behavior *What did you do?*
A relationship ended.	No one will ever love me again. (*All-or-nothing thinking*)	Sad, lonely	Isolated myself so I didn't meet anyone new.
I started drinking or using again.	I will never be sober. (*Magnifying*)	Guilty, discouraged	Kept drinking or using.
My boss told me to do something a certain way.	He thinks he knows it all. (*Jumping to conclusions*)	Angry and frustrated with myself	I didn't listen to him.
	He thinks I am stupid. (*Mind reading*)	Threatened	I started to cry.
	He's an overcontrolling jerk. (*Labeling and mislabeling*)	Angry with the boss, resentful	I did it my way.

In the empty boxes write in some typical situations and behaviors in your own life. Fill in all the columns for each of the examples you provide. These can be situations at home, at work, in the community, or even in this program.

Situation What happened?	Thoughts What did you think?	Feelings How did you feel?	Behavior What did you do?

Feelings Inside and Outside

Sometimes we don't show on the outside how we are feeling on the inside. For example, you may smile at others when you are really feeling sad or scared. Or you may act angry when you are actually feeling vulnerable or scared. Getting your outside self to match your inside self is one way to feel more whole.

Can you recall a time when you felt one way inside but looked different to those around you? Draw or write about your experience below.

Feelings inside:

What you show others:

The DVD of *What I Want My Words To Do To You*

This film was made at the Bedford Hills Prison in the state of New York. A famous writer named Eve Ensler, who wrote the play called *The Vagina Monologues*, ran a writing group for women at Bedford. Although the women in the film are in a prison, their experiences provide us with examples of what can happen when anger escalates or explodes or when anger is misplaced onto another person, and also show us how women can change their lives regardless of the circumstances. Your group will watch parts of the film in various sessions. By the time you complete this program, you will have seen the entire film.

Understanding Keila

In the session, the group used some of the ideas about the inner and outer selves and also about the ways thoughts and feelings can affect behavior, and applied them to Keila's situation. What are your answers to the following questions?

- What were Keila's thoughts that day?

- What was she feeling?

- What did she do?

- We know that values and beliefs, as well as thoughts and feelings, create the inner self. Do we know any more about the values and beliefs in Keila's life?

- How did her inner self—her thoughts, feelings values, and beliefs—affect her behavior?

- What might have been different if she had had a "container" for her feelings?

- How could she have handled the situation differently?

Understanding Me

Think about a time in your life when your anger caused a problem for you. You will realize that your ways of thinking, your assumptions, your values, and your feelings all influenced your behavior. Then begin to fill in the answers to the questions that follow.

- What were your thoughts that day?

- What were some of your beliefs?

- What were you feeling?

- What were your actions?

- How could you have handled the situation differently?

Assignment

1. As you go through the week, focus your awareness on your thinking to see if any of the cognitive distortions the group has discussed occur for you. Keep a record of them here. Try to find one, two, or three occurrences to add to the examples you gave on page 26. Record what you thought, how you felt, and what you did.

2. Think about ways in which you might use the container activity.

3. Finish writing the information about your feelings, beliefs, and actions on pages 30 and 31.

4. What is one thing you will leave this group with: something you have learned or realized?

Feeling Our Feelings

In the last session, you learned that your thoughts can influence your feelings and behaviors. This session focuses on how your feelings can affect your behaviors.

The goals for this session are

- To learn more about our own feelings, including their intensity;
- To learn the five steps to emotional wellness; and
- To understand how our feelings influence our behaviors.

The environment that you are in often affects how you feel. You may be feeling some emotions more often and some less often because of where you are today. Think about the feelings that you have experienced before that you don't typically feel now. Use the space below to write about these "missing" feelings as part of your between-sessions assignment.

Beliefs About Feelings

Here is a list of beliefs about feelings. Make a check mark (√) next to the statements that you have been taught or that you believe.

	There is a right way to feel in every situation.
	If I deny or bury this feeling, it will go away.
	Letting others know that I am feeling bad is weakness.
	Negative feelings are bad and destructive.
	Letting others know what I feel is useless.
	If other people know how I feel, they won't like me.
	Being emotional means being out of control.
	Emotions can just happen for no reason.
	Some emotions are really stupid.
	All painful emotions are the results of a bad attitude.
	If others don't approve of my feelings, I obviously shouldn't feel the way I do.
	Other people are the best judges of how I am feeling.
	Painful emotions are not really important and should be ignored.
	Letting others know how I feel is risky.
	If I feel too good, something bad will happen.

Source: Adapted from *Skills Training Manual for Treating Borderline Personality Disorder*, by M. Linehan, 1993, New York: Guilford Press.

Think of a faulty belief that you have and then think of a recent situation in which the faulty belief came into your mind. How did this belief affect your experience? How did it negatively affect your ability to process your feelings? (Space for writing on next page).

Intensity of Feelings

Feelings occur on a continuum. This means that they have a range of strength, or intensity. For example, if you are afraid, you may feel uneasy or you may feel terrified.

Intensity of Feelings			
Intensity of Feelings	**High**	**Medium**	**Mild**
ANGRY	Irate Furious Enraged Seething	Mad Upset Agitated Disgusted	Uptight Irritated Annoyed Frustrated
AFRAID	Panicky Petrified Terrified Horrified	Scared Fearful Frightened Threatened	Unsure Uneasy Worried Apprehensive
GUILTY	Mortified Sorrowful Worthless Repentant	Regretful Ashamed Remorseful Apologetic	Awkward Unworthy Embarrassed Sorry

Beyond Anger and Violence: A Program for Women

It is normal to feel a variety and range of emotions. Part of healthy living is experiencing and expressing our emotions in healthy ways. A healthy person feels a full range of emotions and is able to cope with intense emotions in a positive way. This can make a big difference in how we feel about ourselves and others. The next activity helps to illustrate the range of some typical emotions.

1. First, consider four common emotions: gladness, sadness, anger, and fear. Choose one color to represent each emotion. Starting on the next page, draw how the intensity of the feeling changes from mild to high (or extreme). Do this for each emotion.

2. After you draw the emotions, write in words that describe the emotions at the different levels of intensity. Look at the following example provided for "gladness" to help you get started.

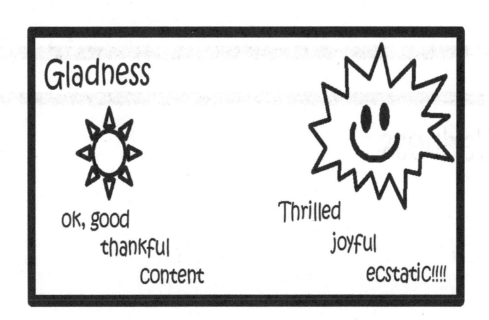

Make your drawings here.

```
┌─────────────────────────────────────┐
│                                     │
│  Gladness                           │
│                                     │
│                                     │
│                                     │
│                                     │
│                                     │
│                                     │
│                                     │
│                                     │
└─────────────────────────────────────┘
```

```
┌─────────────────────────────────────┐
│                                     │
│  Sadness                            │
│                                     │
│                                     │
│                                     │
│                                     │
│                                     │
│                                     │
│                                     │
│                                     │
└─────────────────────────────────────┘
```

Beyond Anger and Violence: A Program for Women

Anger

Fear

Emotional Wellness

We are not born with the ability to handle our emotions. We learn about dealing with our feelings from our families. Many of us grew up in families that did not focus on healthy emotional development. This is something you can learn now. There are five basic steps that can help you begin to create emotional wellness in your life.

Five Steps to Emotional Wellness

1. Become aware of how you are feeling. Tune in to yourself.

2. Try to locate the feeling in your body. Where are you experiencing the sensations?

3. Name the feeling, label it.

4. Express the feeling to yourself or to someone else appropriately.

5. Learn to contain the feeling.

   Step number five is what you have been practicing with the container exercise.

Feelings and the Body

Step two of emotional wellness is having the ability to sense where you feel your feelings in your body.

1. Following your visualization activity, use crayons or colored pencils to show where your feeling is located in your body.

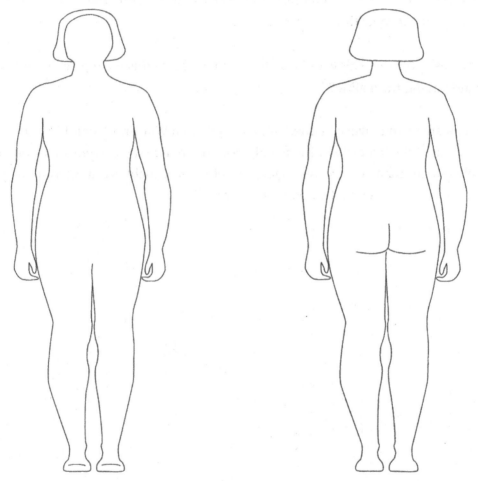

Source: This activity is adapted from *Beyond Trauma: A Healing Journey for Women*, by S. Covington, 2003, Center City, MN: Hazelden.

2. Refer back to the Identifying Feelings list on pages 36 and 37. Pick a feeling from the list that you have felt in the past week or pick a feeling that you have often, even if it isn't on the list. Using a different color, mark on the body illustration where you felt that feeling in your body.

When Feelings Threaten to Overwhelm You

Here are some things to remember when a feeling is overwhelming you:

1. Slow down, or even stop what you are doing.

2. Ask yourself, "What am I feeling?" Try to name the feeling.

3. Ask yourself, "Does the strength or intensity of this feeling match the situation?" Give yourself some time to sort this out.

4. Then ask yourself, "How old do I feel I am as I have this feeling? Is my inner child having the feeling?"

If you are feeling overwhelmed, it is possible that your inner child is connected to the feeling. If the intensity of the feeling does not match the current situation, or you feel younger than your current age, the feeling is probably connected to the past. This is an important clue in dealing with your feelings.

The Observer Self

The Observer Self is a part of you that can help with containment. It is the part of the self that is capable of seeing reality without judging. It observes rather than judges. With practice, you can develop this part of yourself. This is often called *mindfulness*. Mindfulness encourages acceptance rather than avoidance of our experiences and feelings. It helps us develop more flexibility in responding to our emotional experiences.

Following your visualization activity, think about the following:

- How did it feel to be totally in the situation the first time?

- How did it feel to be observing it?

- How did it feel to be in it the second time?

Assignment

1. Go back to the Identifying Feelings list and put circles around the feelings that are most familiar to you.

2. Then, on the side, write the intensity of the way you usually experience each of these feelings: low, medium, or high.

3. Write about the feelings that you have less often now that you are in this program.

4. Work on the body illustrations on page 45. Practice locating your feelings in your body. Use a different color for each feeling you have.

Violence and Trauma in Our Lives

This session focuses on abuse and trauma in women's lives. As you may already know, many women have experienced physical and sexual abuse. Some women also have let their anger get out of control and have used force toward others.

The goals of this session are
- To review the definition of violence,
- To understand the process of trauma, and
- To understand the value of self-soothing and calming techniques.

The self-soothing and calming activities in this program are good for anyone and are especially important if anger, violence, and trauma are part of your history.

Types of Abuse

1. *Emotional abuse* includes name calling, continual criticism, blaming, belittling, embarrassing, humiliating in public or privately, threatening, intimidating, isolating, controlling, withholding approval or affection as punishment, using silence as punishment, withdrawing, playing mind games, manipulating, being inconsistent or unpredictable, breaking promises, abusing pets, manipulating through children, insulting the other's family and/or friends, breaking things, and stalking.

2. *Physical abuse* includes pushing, slapping, kicking, choking, locking out of the house, threatening with a weapon, harassing to the point of physical illness, restraining (for example, by holding someone down or pinning the person's arms), depriving of sleep, withholding food, biting, shaking, spitting, burning, pinching, shooting, stabbing, and deliberately giving someone a sexually transmitted disease.

3. *Sexual abuse* includes rape, coercion, unwanted or inappropriate touching, sexual harassment (including unwanted sexual comments), demanding sex after a beating or illness, sexual criticism, demanding sex in front of others, treating others as sex objects, and nonconsensual sadistic sexual acts. It also includes forced participation in acts the partner objects to, forced intercourse or penetration, and unwanted photographing.

The Process of Trauma

When people are victims of violence or other forms of abuse, they can become traumatized. One definition of trauma is "an external event that overwhelms a person's physical and psychological coping mechanisms or strategies." You can be traumatized by the abuse and violence you commit as well as by what you endure. The diagram on the next page shows the interconnections between events in your life and your thinking, your feeling, your behaviors, and your body's response. All these affect your emotional and physical health.

The Process of Trauma

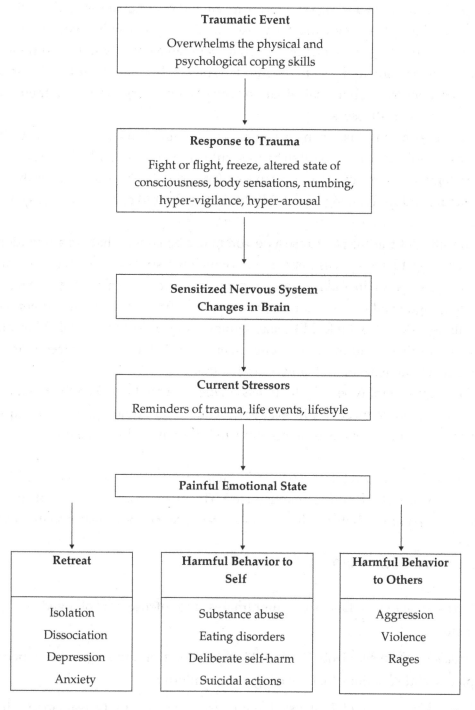

Traumatic Event

Overwhelms the physical and psychological coping skills

Response to Trauma

Fight or flight, freeze, altered state of consciousness, body sensations, numbing, hyper-vigilance, hyper-arousal

Sensitized Nervous System Changes in Brain

Current Stressors

Reminders of trauma, life events, lifestyle

Painful Emotional State

Retreat	**Harmful Behavior to Self**	**Harmful Behavior to Others**
Isolation	Substance abuse	Aggression
Dissociation	Eating disorders	Violence
Depression	Deliberate self-harm	Rages
Anxiety	Suicidal actions	

Source: Adapted from *Beyond Trauma: A Healing Journey for Women*, by S. Covington, 2003, Center City, MN: Hazelden.

The first response that a person has when threatened is to freeze, fight, or run away. This is called the *fight-or-flight* response. Then there are physical and psychological reactions, including hyperarousal, altered consciousness, and numbing. Hyperarousal is a state where the body is agitated and you feel like you are on edge. Altered consciousness is often experienced as being in a daze. Numbing can happen physically in the body and also in the mind, so one feels mentally numb. These are normal reactions to an abnormal situation. The person's nervous system then becomes more vulnerable to stressors.

Trauma also can cause changes in a person's brain chemistry and how the brain functions. People under stress often process information differently. For example, physical, emotional, or sexual abuse can set off a series of physical changes that alter the structure and functioning of a child's brain to help it to cope with a dangerous world.

The stress of trauma can cause a person to use behaviors that are adaptations to the stress. Problems such as dissociation (which is a split between the mind and the body), flashbacks (including fear and terror), and confusion (such as racing or jumbled thoughts) all may stem from the effect of trauma on the brain. Sometimes these things make a person feel like she is going crazy or losing control of her mind. The behaviors that result from these painful emotional states can be placed into three categories: retreat, harm to self, and harm to others.

There are several types of retreat. *Dissociation* is a split between the mind and the body. It can be experienced as physical or psychological numbing. It can be experienced as losing time. This defense mechanism is very useful when a person is being abused.

Anxiety is another retreat response. Women are two to three times more likely to experience anxiety disorders than men are. The most common anxiety disorders for women are panic, phobia (which means intense fear), and posttraumatic stress disorder.

Some of the symptoms of PTSD are

- *Intrusive symptoms*: flashbacks, nightmares, and intense or prolonged distress.

- *Avoidance symptoms*: isolation and disconnection from others; avoiding people, places, and situations that are triggers or reminders.

- *Negative emotions and thoughts*: blaming, excessive negativity, fear, anger, shame, and diminished interests.

Beyond Anger and Violence: A Program for Women

- *Arousal and reactivity*: angry outbursts, reckless and dangerous behavior, hypervigilance, difficulty sleeping, and an increased startle response.

Depression is the third retreat response. It is a condition of feeling persistently sad, having difficulty sleeping and little energy, experiencing loss of hope or joy, having trouble concentrating, experiencing changes in appetite, and/or having frequent thoughts of suicide. The symptoms are present for at least two weeks (usually longer) and often occur as a result of abuse, real or perceived loss, and a feeling of hopelessness that may occur when in a hospital or correctional facility. When someone has severe, chronic depression, she may feel that death is the only solution to the pain.

Depression is different from grief. Grief happens naturally as a result of loss. Grief can be traumatic when the loss comes from a traumatic event.

Isolation is the fourth retreat response. Although we all need some alone time, isolation is different from quiet time alone. Isolation occurs when a woman keeps to herself, avoids interacting with others, and may not even have eye contact with people. In group settings, she will rarely share her feelings or experiences.

Other behaviors that result from trauma are harm to self and harm to others. Women are more likely to retreat or hurt themselves, while men are more likely to engage in aggression and violence as well as to be self-destructive. Women often turn their feelings inward, and men often turn their feelings outward toward others. However, some women's responses to trauma are aggression and violence.

Calming Strategies

Calming, soothing, and grounding activities can help to relax you and keep you in the present moment. There are many different techniques, and some may work better for you than others. Here are some basic ways to calm and ground yourself:

- Reading a book
- Listening to music
- Dancing
- Pacing
- Hugging a stuffed animal or toy
- Taking a shower
- Taking a bubble bath
- Deep breathing
- Eating
- Writing in a journal
- Coloring
- Doing a craft or creative activity
- Calling friends or relatives
- Talking to friends
- Going for a walk in a garden or park
- Exercising
- Doing yoga
- Watching television

Two Calming Activities

Mindful Breathing

1. Slowly take a breath in through your nose. Notice how the breath moves into your lungs, how it feels in your belly, ribs, chest, and shoulders. Notice your belly filling up like a balloon.

2. Exhale slowly. Let the breath move out of your lungs slowly, like a balloon losing air, until they are empty.

3. Repeat this three times.

When you are mindful of your breathing, you can notice whether it is smooth or uneven or barely there. When we pay attention to our breathing, our minds become calmer.

Ten-Point Body Scan (*adapted from M. Napoli, 2006*)

Stand up for this activity.

1. Pay attention to your breathing, as you did before. Notice what is happening in your body.

2. Focus on your feet. Are you leaning on one foot or leaning backward or forward?

3. Focus on your ankles. What do you notice?

4. Focus on your calves and shins. What do you notice?

5. Focus on your knees. Are they locked or relaxed? If they are locked, soften them with a very slight bend.

6. Focus on your thighs, hips, and belly. What do you notice?

7. Focus on your ribs and chest. What do you notice? When you breathe in, does your breath come in easily or does it feel restricted?

8. Focus on your shoulders and arms. What do you notice?

9. Focus on your neck, throat, and head. What do you notice?

10. Focus on your lower, middle, and upper back. What do you notice?

Daily Anger Log

Keep a record of the amount of anger you feel this week. For each day in the week, note how much time you spend being angry. Also note the intensity of your anger. (See Appendix 1 for extra copies of this log.)

Daily Anger Log

Day of Week	What Happened	Intensity of My Anger 1 = Irritated 2 = Somewhat angry 3 = Very angry 4 = Furious/enraged	Amount of Time I Felt Angry
Sunday			
Monday			
Tuesday			
Wednesday			
Thursday			
Friday			
Saturday			

Assignment

1. Before the next session, draw a small picture of your collage. Write about what it means to you.

2. Create a list of calming strategies for yourself.

3. Look back at pages 28 and 29 in this workbook, where you wrote about that fateful day in Keila's life. Review some of the things you noticed and wrote about. Then imagine that Keila had some tools for calming herself and staying in the present. Write about how her behavior might have been different.

4. When you are aware of your thoughts and feelings and know ways to calm or soothe yourself, you have the chance to make choices about your behavior. What if you had had some calming strategies on the day of the event that you discussed earlier? What might have been different? Write about this.

5. Remember to keep a record of when you feel angry and describe it in your Daily Anger Log.

6. Finally, practice the Five Senses activity (on page 6) during the coming week.

The Effects of Trauma

In the last session, we discussed the process of trauma and the importance of using calming and self-soothing techniques. In this session, you will learn more about the effects of trauma on your physical and mental health.

The goals of this session are
- To increase understanding of the effects of trauma on physical health, and
- To increase understanding of the effects of trauma on mental health.

Adverse Childhood Experiences Survey

There are a variety of responses to trauma. There are mental and emotional responses, which occur in the inner self, and there are external responses, which show up in behavior and in physical reactions in the body. One of the most important recent developments in health care is the recognition of the role that serious traumatic experiences play in the development of physical and mental health problems. The following questionnaire can help you to see how trauma may have affected your life.

Take a few minutes to answer "yes" or "no" to the questions below, in terms of your own life history. Please note that the term *household member* in some of the questions means someone *else* in the household when you were growing up.

Adverse Childhood Experiences (ACE) Questionnaire

While you were growing up, during your first 18 years of life:

	Yes	No
1. Did a parent or other adult in the household **often**		
• Swear at you, insult you, put you down, or humiliate you?		
or		
• Act in a way that made you afraid that you might be physically hurt?		
If yes, enter 1	____	____
2. Did a parent or other adult in the household **often**		
• Push, grab, or slap you or throw something at you?		
or		
• **Ever** hit you so hard that you had marks or were injured?		
If yes, enter 1	____	____
	Yes	No
3. Did an adult or person at least 5 years older than you **ever**		
• Touch or fondle you or have you touch his/her body in a sexual way?		
or		
• Try to or actually have oral, anal, or vaginal sex with you?		
If yes, enter 1	____	____

(Continued)

4. Did you **often** feel that

   - No one in your family loved you or thought you were important or special?

   or

   - Your family members didn't look out for one another, feel close to one another, or support one another?

   If yes, enter 1   ____   ____

5. Did you **often** feel that

   - You didn't have enough to eat, had to wear dirty clothes, and had no one to protect you?

   or

   - Your parents were too drunk or high to take care of you or take you to the doctor if you needed it?

   If yes, enter 1   ____   ____

6. Were your parents **ever** separated or divorced?

   If yes, enter 1   ____   ____

7. Was your mother or stepmother

   - **Often** pushed, grabbed, or slapped or had something thrown at her?

   or

   - **Sometimes or often** kicked, bitten, hit with a fist, or hit with something hard?

   or

   - **Ever** repeatedly hit over at least a few minutes or threatened with a gun or knife?

   If yes, enter 1   ____   ____

8. Did you live with anyone who was a problem drinker or alcoholic or who used street drugs?

   If yes, enter 1   ____   ____

(Continued)

The Effects of Trauma   **61**

	Yes	No
9. Was a household member depressed or mentally ill or did a household member attempt suicide?		
If yes, enter 1	____	____
10. Did a household member go to prison?		
If yes, enter 1	____	____

Now add up your "Yes" answers: _____. This is your ACE Score.

The Adverse Childhood Experiences Study

The Adverse Childhood Experiences study shows that the types of experiences described on the survey still have profound effects on people forty and fifty years later. Experiencing these things in childhood puts people at greater risk of having certain physical diseases and mental challenges, even later in life. People who answer "yes" to four or more of the items are at greatest risk for having ongoing health problems, such as heart disease, diabetes, breathing and lung problems, and other conditions (*Felitti & Anda, 2010*).

The ACE study also indicates that a person with a score of four or more "yes" answers is at greater risk for being a substance abuser. Survivors of abuse can become dependent on alcohol and other drugs as a way of managing the effects of trauma and reducing the stress of living in a violent environment. Men who abuse substances are at risk of perpetrating violence against women and children. Women who use substances are more vulnerable to violence—as either victimizers or victims—because of their relationships with others who abuse substances, their impaired judgment while drinking or using, and their being in risky and violence-prone situations. Many women who are not overtly angry when sober find themselves raging when drunk. Many women are under the influence of alcohol or drugs when they commit crimes. There is a cycle of victimization, use of alcohol and/or other drugs, shut down feelings, limited ability to deal with stress, more use of alcohol and/or drugs, and an increased vulnerability to further victimization, as well as to perpetrating abuse.

Beyond Anger and Violence: A Program for Women

The Effects of Trauma and Substance Use on the Brain

The brain is the most complex organ in the body. It directs everything you do, including interpreting and responding to everything you experience.

Trauma affects how the brain functions. People under stress often process and organize information differently than those who are not stressed. The stress of trauma also can result in emotional changes. Problems such as dissociation; flashbacks, including fear and terror; and confusion, such as racing or jumbled thoughts, all may stem from the effect of trauma on the brain.

Alcohol and other drugs also affect the brain. They affect the pathways in the pleasure and reward centers of the brain. Feelings of pain and discomfort are signals from your brain that motivate you to do the things you've learned will make the pain go away. Think about what it feels like after a satisfying meal, a cool drink of water, or a pleasurable sexual experience. Alcohol and other drugs affect these same pleasure and reward centers in the brain. The chemicals in alcohol and other drugs hijack these pathways to reward the repetitive use of the chemical substances, and they cause discomfort when you stop using them. This makes it difficult to experience pleasure from natural behaviors and relationships, as the brain can experience pleasure only when the chemical is present.

This is why addiction can cause people to make irrational, destructive decisions. Everyone who chooses to use a mood-altering substance runs some risk of developing addictive disease, and some people are much more vulnerable than others.

Fifty percent of the risk of becoming addicted is genetic, which means that if addiction runs in your family, your risk of becoming addicted if you choose to use is significantly greater than the risk is for people without this family history. The other 50 percent of risk comes from environmental factors. The list that follows helps to illustrate this.

Risk Factors for Addiction

1. Traumatic or highly stressful childhood experiences

2. Experiencing abuse and violence

3. Early substance use, meaning that the younger you are when you start using alcohol or drugs, the greater the risk of addiction

4. Spending a lot of time around people who use alcohol or other drugs

5. Poor coping mechanisms

6. High levels of stress

7. Poor nutrition

8. Chronic illness, including mental illness such as depression, bipolar disorder, attention deficit disorder (ADD) or attention deficit hyperactivity disorder (ADHD), posttraumatic stress disorder (PTSD) and eating disorders

9. Grief and loss

10. Inability to deal with difficult or painful feelings

Personal Experiences with Substances

These are the questions from your group discussion. You may want to think more about them after the session and make some notes on the next two pages.

- When you think about your life, how do you think that substance use has affected your thinking, feeling, emotions, relationships, choices, and other behaviors?

- What chemicals (alcohol and other drugs) have you used or abused in your life?

- What was going on in your life when you began to use?

- What feelings did the substances give you or what feelings did they help you to medicate or avoid?

- Think specifically about the feeling of anger. Has alcohol or have other drugs increased your anger or lessened it? Do you express anger differently when you are using?

- Think about the genetic and environmental factors that increase the risk of addictive disease. How many of these risks are present in your life?

- What kind of activities and relationships give you natural feelings of pleasure and satisfaction?

- What support do you have for abstinence and self-care?

Beyond Anger and Violence: A Program for Women

Triggers and the Body

During a traumatic event, a person may be so overwhelmed that she can't understand or process what is happening. The unprocessed, emotionally charged bits of trauma can be stored in her memory and in her body. A woman who has experienced the trauma of abuse might be triggered by something such as yelling, a pat down, a large man, or people being too close physically. Triggers also are referred to as *threat clues*. When triggered, the body reacts as though it is re-experiencing the traumatic event, which sets off a reaction of upset, fear, panic, agitation, defensiveness, anger, rage, and perhaps even violence.

What makes you feel scared or upset or angry and could cause you to go into a crisis reaction?

When do you feel overwhelmed? What increases your sense of being overwhelmed?

Here are some typical triggers:

- Lack of privacy
- Not being listened to
- Being teased or picked on
- Feeling criticized
- Feeling humiliated
- Feeling hurt
- Feeling lonely
- Feeling pressured
- Feeling confused
- Darkness
- Loud noises
- People yelling
- Arguments
- Being isolated
- Being touched
- Experiencing unfair treatment
- Not having control
- Having others interfere in plans or goals
- Receiving "mixed" messages
- Being stared at
- Contact with family members

Early warning signs of triggers are physical or emotional signals of distress. If you have been triggered, what did you notice just before losing control?

Here are some warning signs that you may have been triggered (*National Association of State Mental Health Program Directors, 2008*):

- Restlessness
- Agitation
- Pacing
- Shortness of breath
- Increase in body temperature
- Hard breathing
- Tight muscles
- Feeling of being "on edge"
- Sensation of tightness in chest
- Sensation of "knot" in stomach
- Heart pounding
- Sweating
- Teeth clenching
- Hand wringing
- Shaking
- Crying
- Giggling
- Rocking
- Bouncing legs
- Swearing
- Singing inappropriately
- Eating more
- Smoking
- Drinking or using drugs

Yoga Poses and the Mind-Body Connection

Our bodies respond to the ways in which we think, feel, and act. This is called the *mind-body connection*. When a person is stressed, anxious, or upset, her body may try to tell her that something isn't right. The body can do this with aches, pains, and even symptoms of illness. If feelings of stress, sadness, or anxiety are causing physical problems, keeping the feelings inside can make a person feel even worse. The findings of the Adverse Childhood Experiences research demonstrate the mind-body connection.

In addition to the many exercises provided in *Beyond Anger and Violence*, there are certain yoga poses that can help with the release of emotions stored in the body. *Yoga* is the Sanskrit word for "connection." These poses help you to be more consciously aware of your body and your breathing. This is particularly important for women who have histories of abuse and trauma. The four poses suggested are the Breath of Joy, the Seated Pigeon, the Modified Triangle, and the Twisted Branches to Open Wings. These poses are simple to learn, and you can learn to do them by yourself in your living space. See Appendix 3 (page 261) for complete instructions and photographs. Even if these optional yoga poses are not done in your group session, please try them for yourself.

Assignment

1. Record some thoughts about your own triggers. What makes you feel scared or upset or defensive or angry?

2. Look at your Daily Anger Log for this week and fill it in. After you write what happened, add any information about smoking, overeating, and the use of alcohol or other drugs.

Daily Anger Log

Day of Week	What Happened (add any smoking, overeating, and use of alcohol or other drugs)	Intensity of My Anger 1 = Irritated 2 = Mildly angry 3 = Very angry 4 = Furious/enraged	Amount of Time I Felt Angry
Sunday			
Monday			
Tuesday			
Wednesday			
Thursday			
Friday			
Saturday			

3. Also review your work on feelings in the body so that you can better recognize the warning signs when you are being triggered. Make some notes about this.

4. Finally, select your three favorite calming strategies and practice at least two of them in the coming week.

5. Please practice the Breath of Joy yoga pose (p. 261).

Women and Anger

You have been learning about yourself and about your thoughts and feelings and how these affect your behaviors. This session focuses on the feeling of anger. Anger is a particularly complicated feeling. We often think of anger as a negative emotion or "bad" emotion, but feelings are not good or bad. All feelings are clues. Sometimes anger is covering up other feelings that are underneath it, such as hurt, sadness, embarrassment, resentment, envy, and fear of loss. Anger also can be a healthy reaction to a negative or hurtful experience. In creating integrity between our inner and outer selves, we must be willing to explore our anger and how we can best express it.

The goals of this session are

- To better understand the feeling of anger, and
- To discuss self-inflicted violence.

Understanding Our Anger

Anger often happens for one of three reasons:

1. When we sense that an external event, object, or person is threatening or challenging to our ego or pride, our plans, our deeply held beliefs, or our safety.

2. When we experience the frustration of unmet expectations: for example, expectations of how someone else should act or how we want something to happen. Sometimes other people do not even know that we have these expectations or demands.

3. When we are triggered by something that has happened in the past and transfer the emotion from that event to the present situation.

When we sense an external event or person as threatening our physical or emotional well-being, an internal reaction starts. First we make assumptions about the possible danger of the frustration or threat. If we decide that it is not very great or that we can deal with it successfully, we can remain calm and unflustered. But if we decide that we cannot handle the threat, anger emerges in an effort to reduce or destroy the threat and protect our expectations or our egos or our moral standards or our physical selves.

Well-channeled anger can motivate us to resolve conflicts, to address social injustice, and to overcome life's obstacles. So we don't want to eliminate all anger. However, anger often is connected to aggressive or violent behavior. When we don't know how to express anger appropriately, that's when we get into trouble. The anger is not a problem, but how we deal with it may be a problem.

Men and women often are raised to express anger differently. Many females are taught that expressing anger is "unladylike," although it is accepted behavior in males. Some women misdirect their anger and it comes out as mean gossip, sulking, or never speaking to someone again. In creating integrity or connection between our inner and outer selves, we must be willing to explore our anger and how we can best express it.

Words for Anger

Following is a list of words related to anger. It may be similar to the one your group created. Please add any words that have meaning for you.

Aggravation	Ferocity	
Agitation	Frustration	
Annoyance	Fury	
Bitterness	Hatred	
Contempt	Hostility	
Cruelty	Irritation	
Destructive	Jealousy	
Disgust	Mean spirited	
Dislike	Outrage	
Embarrassment	Rage	
Envy	Resentment	
Exasperation	Spite	

Meeting a Feeling

The visualization activity was designed to help you to explore your inner self and to look specifically at the feeling of anger.

1. As you think about this experience, draw a picture of your anger—the feeling you met.

2. What did you learn from the feeling? Make notes about your answers to the following questions:

   • What does your anger do for you?

   • What does it need from you?

The Anger Funnel

People who realize early in life that it is often not safe to express their fear, hurt, or sadness often learn to put anger in place of these other feelings. They use what is called the *anger funnel*. We pour a lot of different emotions into this funnel, and anger is the only thing that comes out the other end. The anger that emerges from the funnel exists on an imaginary line ranging from silence and isolation to rage and violence. One end of the line is silent, controlled, and passive; the other end is reactive, out of control, and explosive.

Of course, we all feel anger at various times. It is how we react to the anger that matters. This is why it's important to understand the thoughts and feelings underneath our anger, so that we can express and deal with our anger appropriately.

1. Think about a situation in which you were angry. At the bottom of the funnel on the next page, write in the words that describe your anger.

2. What other feelings were there, perhaps before the anger? Put these at the top end of the funnel. (See the example below.)

Example

Hurt, Sadness, Fear, Insecurity

Anger, Rage, and Violence

The Anger Funnel

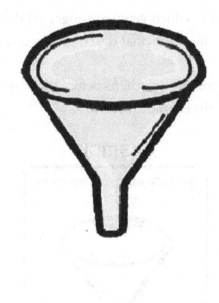

Do you see how this happens?

Beyond Anger and Violence: A Program for Women

Anger Triggers

Here are a few examples of things that may cause someone to become angry. Take a few moments to write in some of the things in both categories that make you angry.

Interpersonal

- A certain person's (particular) behavior
- Being talked to in a patronizing manner
- Being kept waiting
- Being treated unfairly
- Harassment
- _____
- _____
- _____
- _____

General

- Loud noise
- Mechanical things that don't work
- Confusing directions or instructions
- Damage to my property
- _____
- _____
- _____
- _____

Hidden Anger

Sometimes anger is hidden, and you may not recognize it. Unrecognized anger can be damaging because it ultimately is expressed in indirect and often inappropriate ways. The following is a list of things that may be signals of bottled-up, negative emotions.

Signs of Hidden Anger

____ 1. Avoiding starting or finishing tasks

____ 2. Aeing late in certain situations

____ 3. Using hurtful humor

____ 4. Making sarcastic or flip comments

____ 5. Smiling when you don't feel happy

____ 6. Being bored or losing interest in things you are usually enthusiastic about

____ 7. Getting tired more easily than usual

____ 8. Being overly upset about little things

____ 9. Feeling "road rage"

____ 10. Difficulty sleeping

____ 11. Clenching your jaws, especially while sleeping

____ 12. Grinding your teeth, especially while sleeping

____ 13. Feeling down for no particular reason

____ 14. Chronic depression

____ 15. Anxiety attacks

____ 16. High blood pressure

____ 17. Getting stomach pains or ulcers

____ 18. Engaging in self-inflicted violence

Have you experienced any of these things? Make a check mark next to the ones that you have experienced.

Did you know that these were signs of hidden anger?

Self-Inflicted Violence

Some women cut or burn themselves as a way to try to numb or control the pain of abuse. Most of the women who do this try to keep it a secret. If this is an issue for you please talk to a counselor to help you learn other coping mechanisms.

Here are some reasons why women might begin to physically hurt themselves:

1. To distract themselves from emotional pain
2. To mark or scar the body
3. To let something bad out
4. To keep from hurting someone else
5. To express anger indirectly
6. To relieve anger
7. To gain or reclaim control of the body
8. To punish themselves
9. To relieve tension and anxiety
10. To feel real by feeling pain or seeing the injury
11. To feel calm or numb by giving some release
12. To experience an increase in endorphins and the euphoria, or high, that goes with it
13. To express feelings of isolation and alienation
14. As a response to self-hatred or guilt
15. To communicate their pain and anger to others
16. To nurture themselves or seek nurturing for their injuries

Personal Anger Inventory

Below is a Personal Anger Inventory. Write some notes in response to each set of items listed. This will help you to remember the things that you have learned in Session Five.

Personal Anger Inventory

1. How often do I feel angry?

   _____ Most of the time

   _____ At least once each day

   _____ Two or three times per week

   _____ About once a week

   _____ Rarely

   _____ _____

   _____ _____

   _____ _____

2. When I am angry, I usually feel

   _____ Annoyed

   _____ Irritated

   _____ Vexed or peeved

   _____ Frustrated

   _____ Resentful

   _____ Furious

   _____ Tense

   _____ Afraid

   _____ Depressed

   _____ Out of control

   _____ Dangerous

_____ _____

_____ _____

_____ _____

3. When I am angry, I usually do this

_____ Get quiet

_____ Keep it to myself

_____ Sulk or pout

_____ Avoid others

_____ Cry

_____ Swear

_____ Hold on to resentments/grudges

_____ Vow to get even

_____ Do deep breathing

_____ Try to relax and calm down

_____ Yell or scream at someone

_____ Throw something

_____ Break something

_____ Hit someone

_____ Drink

_____ Use drugs

_____ Hurt myself

_____ _____

_____ _____

_____ _____

4. I often express anger through

_____ Sarcasm

_____ Belittling or putting down

_____ Gossip or backstabbing

_____ Blaming others

_____ Bullying

_____ Trying to control others

_____ Raising my voice

_____ Physical abuse

_____ Pain or illnesses in my body

_____ _____

_____ _____

_____ _____

5. After I feel angry, then I feel

_____ Tense or nervous

_____ Embarrassed

_____ Ashamed

_____ Exhausted

_____ Helpless

_____ Powerful

_____ Guilty

_____ Depressed

_____ _____

_____ _____

_____ _____

6. I have used anger to

_____ Survive

_____ Get what I want

_____ Intimidate others

_____ Control others

_____ Make me feel "alive"

_____ Hide other feelings

_____ _____

_____ _____

_____ _____

7. Based on what I now know about my anger, I would describe my anger style as (refer to your notes on pages 14 and 15)

_____ Anger avoidant (When I feel anger, I try to ignore it or contain it.)

_____ Anger reactive (When I feel anger, I feel the need to express it immediately.)

8. How is my way of handling anger effective?

9. How is my way of handling anger ineffective?

- *If you are anger avoidant*: Turning my anger on myself has hurt me by

- *If you are anger reactive*: I have directed my anger toward others and hurt them by

10. If I use alcohol or other drugs, it affects my anger by

11. If I were less angry, what would replace my anger?

Assignment

1. Look at the Five Steps to Emotional Wellness on page 44. Pick a situation in which you have felt or currently feel anger and then review the five steps in relation to this feeling of anger.

2. If you are angry this week, and the intensity of the anger doesn't match the situation, ask yourself what might be beneath the anger. Here are some clues:

   • How old do you feel?

   • Is the anger a familiar feeling?

   • Is it appropriate to the situation?

Try to make some notes here about this.

3. Finish filling out your Personal Anger Inventory as best you can at this time.

4. *Optional*: Keep your Daily Anger Log for this week. After you write what happened, add any information about smoking, overeating, and the use of alcohol or other drugs. (There are additional copies in Appendix 1 if the Log is helpful and you would like to continue using it.)

Daily Anger Log

Day of Week	What Happened (add any smoking, overeating, and use of alcohol or other drugs)	Intensity of My Anger 1 = Irritated 2 = Mildly angry 3 = Very angry 4 = Furious/enraged	Amount of Time I Felt Angry
Sunday			
Monday			
Tuesday			
Wednesday			
Thursday			
Friday			
Saturday			

Tools for Managing Anger

When we spend some time observing ourselves and doing what is called self-reflection, we understand ourselves better. Now that you understand the emotion of anger better, you can learn some tools and strategies for recognizing and managing your anger. This new learning can be used to help you manage your emotional life and get closer to being your personal best.

The goals of this session are

- To learn tools for anger management, and
- To practice self-reflection in order to monitor how we are feeling and functioning.

Anger Management Strategies

Here are a variety of ideas, or strategies, you can use when you feel angry:

1. Accept anger as a normal emotion. Try not to feel guilty for feeling angry.

2. Learn to identify your triggers.

3. Learn to recognize old anger as opposed to current anger.

4. Try to identify the feelings underneath the anger.

5. Stop and think before reacting to your anger.

6. Give yourself a "cool down" period when you are feeling intense anger.

7. Use the Creating a Container technique or another form of "time out."

8. Instead of "stuffing" angry feelings, talk to someone.

9. Take responsibility for your actions and choices. Do not blame others.

10. Share feelings in a direct, respectful way.

11. Accept that there are things you can't change or control.

12. Make a decision to manage your anger, rather than letting it manage you.

In the activity that follows, rate yourself on whether you use the ideas listed for managing your anger. Circle the appropriate number. On the scale of 1 to 5, a 1 means you never do it, and a 5 means that you always do it. You may be somewhere in between.

Strategies for Managing Anger

		Never				Always
1. Accept anger as a normal emotion. Try not to feel guilty for feeling angry.		1	2	3	4	5
2. Learn to identify your triggers.		1	2	3	4	5
3. Learn to recognize old anger as opposed to current anger.		1	2	3	4	5
4. Try to identify the feelings underneath the anger.		1	2	3	4	5
5. Stop and think before reacting to your anger.		1	2	3	4	5
6. Give yourself a "cool down" period when you are feeling intense anger.		1	2	3	4	5
7. Use the Creating a Container technique or another form of "time out."		1	2	3	4	5
8. Instead of "stuffing" angry feelings, talk to someone.		1	2	3	4	5
9. Take responsibility for your actions and choices. Do not blame others.		1	2	3	4	5
10. Share feelings in a direct, respectful way.		1	2	3	4	5
11. Accept that there are things you can't change or control.		1	2	3	4	5
12. Make a decision to manage your anger, rather than letting it manage you.		1	2	3	4	5

Anger Dos and Don'ts

Anger Dos and Don'ts

This is an important list of dos and don'ts. Mark which ones you are doing now.

____ 1. Do ask yourself, "Why am I angry?"

____ 2. Don't react while you are in the heat of the anger. First, cool down.

____ 3. Do take time out to think about the problem and understand your position. Ask yourself:

- What is it that makes me angry?
- What is the real issue here?
- Where do I stand?
- What do I want to accomplish?
- Who is responsible for what?
- What, specifically, do I want to change?

(Continued)

_____ 4. Don't use "below-the-belt" tactics, including blaming, interpreting, diagnosing, labeling, analyzing, preaching, moralizing, ordering, warning, interrogating, ridiculing, threatening, and lecturing.

_____ 5. Do speak up when an issue is important to you. Let the rest go.

_____ 6. Do make rules with your partner (and others) and follow them (for example, no yelling, name-calling, or bringing up problems at bedtime).

_____ 7. Do try to avoid speaking for another person. For example, if you are angry with your partner's actions, don't say, "I think our daughter felt terrible when you didn't find the time to come to her basketball game." Instead, say, "I was upset when you didn't come. You are important to me, and I really wanted you there."

_____ 8. Do try to make clear, specific requests rather than vague ones.

_____ 9. Don't participate in intellectual arguments that go nowhere. Don't waste time trying to convince others that you are right. Instead, you may want to say, "Well, it may not make sense to you, but this is how I feel."

_____ 10. Don't tell another person what she or he thinks or feels or "should" think or feel.

_____ 11. Do try saying, "I need to give myself a time-out from the conversation. We can talk later when we are both calm."

_____ 12. Do try to accept and appreciate the fact that people are different.

_____ 13. Do recognize that each person is responsible for his or her own behavior.

_____ 14. Don't expect change to come about from "hit-and-run" confrontations. Change occurs slowly in relationships. Even the small changes you make will be tested many times to see if you really mean them.

_____ 15. Do consider timing and tact when bringing up a "high-twitch" issue.

_____ 16. Do apologize for your part of a problem or fight, even if you secretly believe it's only 2 percent.

_____ 17. Do exit a conversation if you're on the receiving end of demeaning or insulting behavior.

Source: Adapted from _The Dance of Anger: A Woman's Guide to Changing the Patterns of Intimate Relationships_, by H. Lerner, 2005 (Rev. ed.), New York: HarperCollins.

Working on this is an important part of the assignment because it will help you to focus on the feeling of anger and the strategies you want to practice and develop for managing it.

Self-Reflection Tool

Here is a tool you can use to monitor how you are feeling and functioning. This will let you know when you need to use caution because you are moving out of optimal functioning and away from your personal best. Notice that there is a place for you to add the names of people you want to talk to when you are moving away from your personal best.

Use this tool twice each day for the next two weeks. (There are additional Self-Reflection Tools in Appendix 2, pages 251–260.)

Self-Reflection Tool

This Self-Reflection Tool will help you monitor how you are doing (on the outside) and feeling (on the inside). Take time each morning and evening to fill it in.

1. First, write words that describe *My Personal Best*, *Stressed*, and *Overwhelmed* in the blanks under each term. (See the sample word bank that follows.)

2. In the squares on the chart on page 97, use the colors green (*My Personal Best*), yellow (*Stressed*), and red (*Overwhelmed*) to show how you are doing and feeling at the moment.

3. Write a number between 1 (doing and feeling very poorly) and 10 (doing and feeling very well) to indicate your approximate level of well-being, and also write two words that reflect how you are doing and feeling at the moment. (See the example on next page of how to fill in the squares.)

4. If I am below 5, I will share with _____ or _____ or _____.

This tool allows you to capture, record, and create awareness about your own rhythm and flow of energy over time. The goal is to be honest and self-aware. No one is in the green (at their personal best) all the time; that is not the expectation.

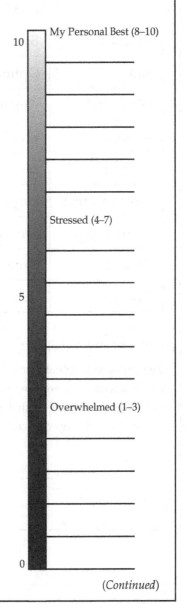

(Continued)

Sample Word Bank

How are you feeling and functioning? Here are some words that women have suggested in describing their *My Personal Best*, *Stressed*, and *Overwhelmed* feelings. Feel free to use any words you like. You also can add your own words to this list.

Blessed	Fussy	Tired	Mindful	Balanced
Grouchy	Closed off	Tremendous	Good	Unbalanced
Irritated	Open-minded	Exhausted	Confused	Loud
Shocked	Bored	Worried	Motivated	Quiet
Sad	Optimistic	Content	Happy	Proud
Wonderful	Anxious	Stupendous	Sad	Hopeful
In pain	Positive	Graceful	Shady	Determined
Energetic	Lonely	Loved	Pissed off	Hungry
Overwhelmed	Surprised	Humble	Excited	Angry
Discouraged	Sensitive	Appreciative	Frustrated	Grateful
Ecstatic	Smug	Beautiful	Helpful	Appalled
Squirrely	Sexy	Lustful	Baffled	Revengeful

Example of filled-in squares:

Remember to fill in both the color and the number to describe how you are feeling in the morning and in the evening (with the date). Also add words to describe how you feel.

Date

5/1	5/2

AM

6	3.5
Excited	Anxious
Nervous	Scared

(Continued)

Beyond Anger and Violence: A Program for Women

Self Reflection Tool

Date						
AM						
PM						

Date						
AM						
PM						

If I am below 5, I will share with _____ or _____ or _____.

Reflection

(To be completed when your chart is full)

What have I learned from my self-reflection?

Will this help me move forward? How?

Taking Responsibility for Sharing

(Prior to sharing when you are below 5)

Think of whom you will share with and the impact this will have on that person or those persons. Think about what and how you will share in a way that will not "contaminate" the other person(s) or be a way for you to get the other person(s) to "take your side."

Remember, the goal is for you to get clear and reduce your stress level.

Sometimes just being heard is enough. At other times, you may come up with an action plan to help reduce your stress level.

Source: "Self-Reflection Tool," by Lorraine Robinson, 2013 (unpublished).

My Personal Best

In your group activity, you imagined your life without the kind of anger that is destructive to you and others.

1. In order to make this happen, what do you need to stop doing?

2. What will you do instead?

3. Which of the tools you are learning are working for you?

4. How will you continue to do these things that are working?

When anger no longer dominates your life, there is space for other feelings, such as acceptance, calmness, inner strength, peace, joy, and happiness. This is when you are at your personal best.

Are you ready to make a commitment to changing your anger?

Assignment

1. Look at the list of Strategies for Managing Anger on which you rated yourself, starting on page 93. Try to practice one or two of these strategies during the week and improve your rating.

2. Pick one of the don'ts from the list of Dos and Don'ts on pages 93 and 94 and try to stop doing it.

3. Try to use one of your do's more often this week.

4. Use the Self-Reflection Tool twice each day, in the morning and evening. Rate yourself, and note when you are moving into the caution area. Remember to speak to the people you have selected and get their help.

Understanding Ourselves

In this session, you continue to explore issues related to the individual, or the *self*, looking at the inner self and the outer self and at the process of integration, or wholeness.

The goals of this session are

- To better understand anger, aggression, and violence; and
- To integrate some of the materials from earlier sessions in order to understand what it means to become a whole person.

DVD of *What I Want My Words To Do To You*

Your group has discussed how thoughts and feelings influence behaviors. Today, you used Keila's story as an example.

- What was Keila feeling?

- What she was thinking?

- What were some of her beliefs?

- How did her trauma influence her behavior?

- How was anger involved?

- What were some of her triggers?

- Was substance abuse involved? If so, how did it affect the situation?

- What could Keila have changed in her behavior? How could she have handled the situation differently?

- What other options did she have for her behavior?

Understanding My Anger

Think of a situation or event in your life in which your feeling of anger and your angry reaction caused problems for you and others. You may want to use some of the answers from the activity on pages 30 and 31. You may have some different things to add.

- Why were you angry?

- What were your thoughts at that time?

- What were your feelings?

- What were some of your beliefs?

- Were there things that acted as "triggers" for you? What were they?

- Did trauma influence your behavior? If so, how?

- Rate your anger on a scale of 1 to 10 by circling a number.

  1   2   3   4   5   6   7   8   9   10

- Was substance abuse involved? How did it affect the situation?

- What action did you take?

- What could you have done to change your behavior that could have changed the outcome? How could you have handled the situation differently?

Understanding My Behavior

If we are not aware of our thoughts, feelings, triggers, and motivations, we risk doing the same things over and over, even if they don't get us the results we want or are harmful. The table that follows helps to describe Keila's motivations and behavior. You can use it as a sample to help you fill out your own table on the next page. This activity will help you to see that many different parts of yourself are interconnected.

Understanding Keila

Situation or event	Keila's rape
Her feelings	Sadness, fear, betrayal, anger, confusion
Her thoughts	Wanting answers
Distorted thinking	It is safe if I have a gun.
Her behavior	Shooting him
Alternative behavior	Trusting her instincts that he was not safe and trying to find someone safe to talk to

If we are aware of how we think and what we are feeling, we have more choices about how we interpret and deal with situations. You can use this activity repeatedly to help you understand different events in your life.

Understanding Me

Situation or event	
Your feelings	
Your thoughts	
Distorted thinking	
Your behavior	
Alternative behavior	

Becoming Whole

Earlier in the program, the phrase "whole people with integrity" was used to describe what happens when there is harmony and agreement between your inner self (your thoughts, feelings, beliefs, and values) and your outer self (your behavior and relationships). One definition of *integrity* is "the state of being whole." As part of the upward growth spiral, which is expanding away from violence, you are learning concepts and tools that will help you to connect, or integrate, your inner and outer selves.

Try to answer the following questions as honestly as possible. Take as much time as you need to continue working on these questions throughout this program.

1. What do I believe in?

2. What kind of person do I want to become?

If you think back to the beginning of this program, one of the goals mentioned was to be part of a group of women committed to making the world less violent. You can start to do that by beginning to change yourself. An important piece of this work is creating inner peace. Using self-calming techniques, such as relaxation exercises, breathing exercises, and meditation, can help you to do that. Yoga helps, too.

Assignment

1. Continue to work on the activities on pages 104, 105, and 107. These will help you to understand yourself and your behavior better.

2. Finish answering the two questions on pages 108 and 109 about what you believe in and what kind of person you want to become. You may find that you gain new insights about these during the week.

3. Fill in your Self-Reflection Tool again, twice each day, during the coming week.

4. Think about the concept of inner peace and what might help that to happen for you.

Relationships

Our Families

Session Eight begins the second part of the *Beyond Anger and Violence* program. Your group has discussed the four areas, or layers, of our lives that create the risks for violence; these are the individual, relationship, community, and societal areas. Part B of the program looks at how our relationships with our friends, intimate partners, and family members increase our risk of becoming victims of violence or of directing aggressive or violent behavior toward others.

The topic of Session Eight is the source of some of your most influential relationships: your family.

The goals for this session are

- To understand various family dynamics, and
- To understand the influences of our families on our lives, especially when anger, aggression, and violence are present.

Self-Soothing Activity: Deep Breathing

Doing a relaxation exercise is one of the best ways to calm and soothe yourself. Deep breathing is a well-known relaxation technique. You will be practicing this during each session in this part of the program.

1. Close your eyes or lower your eyelids.

2. Take a deep breath in while you silently count to four.

3. Now begin breathing out slowly while you silently count to four. Try to breathe deeply from within your abdomen, rather than higher in your chest.

4. Breathe in again while counting.

5. And breathe out again.

6. Repeat the slow breathing six more times. Count to four with each breath.

Risk Factors

One of the most influential relationships in anyone's life is her relationship with the family she grows up in. Whether it is a birth family or a foster family, our experiences there mold who we become. Unfortunately, some families contain several risk factors for aggression and violence. One or both of the parents may be constantly angry. There may be some type of abuse between the parents or toward the children. Even having a poor relationship with a parent or having violent friends can influence whether a young person engages in or becomes a victim of violence. As we grow, our personal relationships with our peers, friends, and intimate partners also influence the risks of our becoming victims or victimizers (perpetrators of violence).

Here are some risk factors in relationships (*Dahlberg & Krug, 2002*):

- Poor parenting
- Marital problems

- Violent parental conflict

- Low socioeconomic household status

- Friends that engage in violence

Socioeconomic means the combination of factors in the society, such as race and class status, with the economic factors that are also present, such as income, savings, and the availability of jobs.

Family Sculpture

Doing a family sculpture is a way to look at how certain things happen in a family. Almost none of us grew up in an ideal family. Many families struggle with multiple challenges. In the United States, a family with two adults who are the parents of all the children is now in the minority. So there may be the additional challenges of having a single-parent family or a blended family.

In some families, the members hide behind roles that help them to survive and get their basic needs met in emotionally confusing environments. These roles limit people's ability to feel or to listen to *internal* clues because the roles are responses to *external* clues.

Our roles were important to our survival as children, but most of us carry the roles into adulthood, even though they have outlived their usefulness and may have little connection to who we are now.

When we think about what we learned about parenting from our parents, we can realize what we want to do the same or differently with our own children and other family members. In the session, you discussed your reactions and insights as a result of the Family Sculpture activity. What were some of your thoughts and insights?

The Cost of Violence

The drawing below shows how a woman growing up in a violent family can develop posttraumatic stress disorder, or PTSD. At first, she may feel shock, numbness, anxiety, a sense of powerlessness, shame, irritability, sadness, and anger. If the violence continues, her symptoms may become more severe, debilitating, and prolonged. She may develop chronic PTSD, with symptoms such as numbing, a sense of re-experiencing the abuse, hyperarousal or agitation, and negative feelings and thoughts.

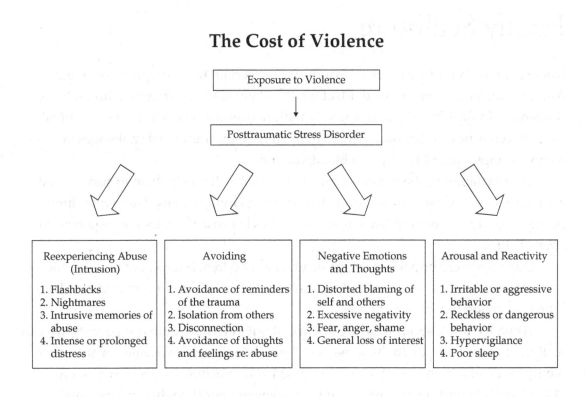

The Cost of Violence

Exposure to Violence

Posttraumatic Stress Disorder

Reexperiencing Abuse (Intrusion)	Avoiding	Negative Emotions and Thoughts	Arousal and Reactivity
1. Flashbacks 2. Nightmares 3. Intrusive memories of abuse 4. Intense or prolonged distress	1. Avoidance of reminders of the trauma 2. Isolation from others 3. Disconnection 4. Avoidance of thoughts and feelings re: abuse	1. Distorted blaming of self and others 2. Excessive negativity 3. Fear, anger, shame 4. General loss of interest	1. Irritable or aggressive behavior 2. Reckless or dangerous behavior 3. Hypervigilance 4. Poor sleep

Which of these things have you experienced?

Feelings and the Family

Some families have unspoken rules about feelings, such as "Act happy, no matter what." Take some time to describe the unspoken rules in the home when you were growing up. What were the feelings and behaviors that were okay? What was not okay?

Unspoken Rules

Describe the feelings that you were free to express and the behaviors and/or experiences that you could share.	Describe the feelings and behaviors that you learned to keep hidden.
Example: happiness	*Example: loneliness*

The Family Anger Questionnaire

This questionnaire helps you to explore what you learned about anger when you were growing up. It also will help you to describe how you deal with anger now and how you want to express angry feelings in the future.

The Family Anger Questionnaire: 1. The Past

1. When you were growing up, how did your mother (or primary caregiver or role model) act when she was angry? How did she express her anger?

2. How did she respond to your anger?

3. When you were growing up, what did your father (or other caregiver or role model) do when he was angry? How did he express his anger?

118

4. How did he respond to your anger?

5. As a child, what did you learn about how you could express your anger? How did you express your anger?

6. How did other family members express their anger?

Source: Adapted from *In Quest of the Mythical Mate*, by E. Bader & P. T. Pearson, 1988, New York: Brunner/Mazel.

The Family Anger Questionnaire: 2. The Present and the Future

1. In the present, what do you do when you are angry with someone who is close to you?

2. Are you satisfied with how you resolve your anger with others?

3. You were asked earlier if you were willing to consider the possibility of changing how you express your anger. Based on previous sessions of this program and your self-reflection, how ready do you feel to make this change? Why?

4. What have you decided to change so that you will feel better about how you resolve anger with others who are close to you? Describe what the changes will look like in terms of your behavior. What will be different? How will it feel?

5. How important is this to you? Why is it important?

Source: Adapted from *In Quest of the Mythical Mate*, by E. Bader & P. T. Pearson, 1988, New York: Brunner/Mazel.

Wheel of the Nurturing Family

The family sculpture gives you an idea of what happens in a troubled family. What happens in a nurturing family? Look at the Wheel of the Nurturing Family below.

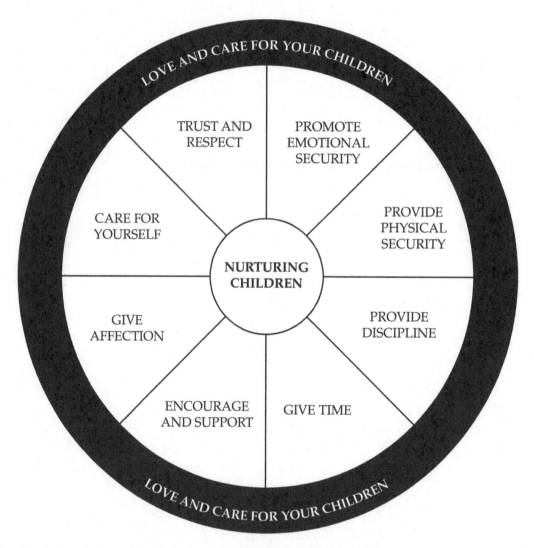

Source: Duluth Domestic Abuse Intervention Project, 202 East Superior Street, Duluth, MN 55802.

Beyond Anger and Violence: A Program for Women

1. **I promote your emotional security.**

   - I talk and act in ways that encourage you to feel safe and comfortable in expressing yourself.

   - I am gentle with you.

   - I am dependable. You can count on me. You know I am here for you.

2. **I provide physical security for you.**

   - I provide you with food, shelter, and clothing.

   - I teach you about personal hygiene and healthy nutrition.

   - I watch out for your safety.

   - I make sure that we have a predictable family routine.

   - If you are hurt, I make sure your injuries are taken care of.

3. **I provide you with appropriate discipline.**

   - I am consistent and predictable.

   - I make sure that rules are appropriate for your age and abilities.

   - I am clear about limits and expectations so that you know what is expected of you.

   - I view and use discipline as a learning experience, not only as punishment.

4. **I give you my time.**

   - I participate in your life: your activities, school, sports, special events and days, celebrations, and friends.

   - I include you appropriately in my activities.

   - I share who I am with you.

5. **I encourage and support you.**

   - I validate you so that you feel seen and heard by me.

   - I encourage you to follow your interests.

   - I acknowledge that you may disagree with me, and I listen when you do.

   - I recognize and acknowledge when you have improved.

   - I teach you new skills.

   - It's okay if you make mistakes. We all make mistakes and can learn from them.

6. **I give you affection.**

   - I am affectionate with you, both in words and in my actions.

   - You feel safe to be affectionate with me.

   - I take care of you and show affection when you are physically or emotionally hurt.

7. **I take care of myself. This helps me to take better care of you.**

   - I take personal time for myself.

   - I take care of my health.

   - My friendships are important to me, and I stay connected with friends.

   - I accept love from others.

8. **I give you trust and respect.**

   - I acknowledge and respect your right to have your own feelings, friends, activities, and opinions.

   - I support your independence.

   - I allow you to have privacy.

   - I respect your feelings for your other parent.

   - I believe you.

This wheel can help to provide an example of what you may have missed. It also can be a model for the type of family you want to create.

Beyond Anger and Violence: A Program for Women

Assignment

1. In the Unspoken Rules activity, finish writing in the feelings and behaviors that were okay and not okay to express in the family you grew up in. Remember to include the feeling of anger.

2. Then, on pages 118 to121, complete the Anger Questionnaires for the past and the present and future.

3. Finally, think about and try to answer this question: If I had grown up in a nurturing family, how would this affect my adult relationships?

Communication

Communication is important because it is a key to expressing who you are and it directly affects your relationships with others. This session focuses on different communication styles, on skills to improve communication, and on the importance of communicating your emotions in a relationship.

The goals of this session are
- To convey the importance of clear communication,
- To develop basic communication skills, and
- To practice communicating emotions.

Communication Styles

People communicate with one another in a variety of ways. One of the first places where we learn about communication is in our families. Sometimes we get into the habit of communicating in a particular way. The following are four typical ways of communicating.

1. Passive Communication

This could be apologizing a lot without expressing feelings, needs, or ideas; using a weak, hesitant voice; looking down when talking; using poor eye contact; having poor posture; or letting others make decisions for you.

An example is: "I thought that maybe . . . you could . . . maybe, um . . ."

2. Aggressive Communication

This could be bossing people around, acting in a way that says that other people's ideas and opinions don't matter, speaking in a loud and demanding voice, "staring down" the person you're talking to, or having clenched hands and a stiff posture.

An example is: "You idiot, what were you thinking?"

3. Passive-Aggressive Communication

This could be trying to get people to do what you want by being indirect or not being "straight up," using disguised resistance, putting things off until later, or being stubborn. It can be saying that you will do something and then not doing it, while knowing ahead of time that you aren't going to do it.

Two examples are: "Go ahead and go to the movie; I'll just sit home alone," and, "I guess you're just doing what you have to do, but I thought you were my friend."

4. Assertive Communication

This includes direct, clear, and honest communication; using a voice that is firm but respectful; making eye contact without staring; and keeping the hands and body relaxed.

An example is: "I need you to tell me what's going on so I can understand what you need."

Nonverbal Communication

In your session, you did an activity that demonstrated the power of nonverbal communication. What were some of your group's reactions to this activity?

What particular thing(s) did you learn from this activity?

Communicating Emotions

Being able to communicate your feelings is an aspect of emotional wellness. Usually, we learn how and whether to communicate our feelings in our families of origin. What was your reaction to hearing about

- Trying to guess what is going on when people don't communicate directly and openly?

- Only talking about "non-risky" facts?

- Stating opinions as facts?

- "Poor me, ain't it awful" stories?

How did it feel to share a feeling of sadness?

How did it feel to share something that you feel angry about?

How did it feel to share something that has given you a feeling of joy?

How did it feel to be interrupted?

Strategies for Creating Connection in Communication

Good communication involves both listening and sharing. Below is a list of ideas or strategies for creating connection through effective communication. You may want to add others from your group discussion.

- Maintaining eye contact
- Giving the speaker your full attention
- Listening to what the other person is saying (instead of planning your response)
- Allowing others to complete their statements (not interrupting)
- Staying present
- Using "I" statements
- Being honest
- Not screaming or yelling
- Asking questions for clarification
- Restating to the other person what you have heard, to demonstrate that you understand her
- Not prejudging
- Being assertive without being aggressive
- Avoiding passive-aggressive communication

Responses to Stress

For each statement below, circle a number from 1 to 5 to indicate your common response when you are stressed but need to communicate. A 1 means that you seldom do this, and a 5 means that you do it often.

Under stress, I usually	Seldom				Often
Stop thinking	1	2	3	4	5
Think negative thoughts about myself	1	2	3	4	5
Think negative thoughts about others	1	2	3	4	5
Feel angry at others and express it instantly without thinking	1	2	3	4	5
Shut down and feel nothing	1	2	3	4	5

When I am under stress, here is what I want to

1. Understand about myself:

2. Understand about the situation:

3. Give up or stop doing:

Assignment

1. Practice at least one of the strategies for creating connection in communication that were listed in the group session and/or practice sharing your feelings with someone you trust.

2. Practice the Seated Pigeon pose (see Appendix 3).

3. Because stress often creates negative, incorrect beliefs about oneself and others, it will be helpful for you to fill in the following boxes as part of your assignment.

When I'm under stress and have difficulty communicating, these are some of my common thoughts:	
Three of my negative thoughts about myself or others	Three positive statements about myself or others that I can use to soothe myself
1.	1.
2.	2.
3.	3.

Beyond Anger and Violence: A Program for Women

Power and Control

It is important to understand power and control, particularly in abusive or violent relationships, and how they affect women's lives.

The goals of this session are
- To understand the uses of power and control in relationships, and
- To explore what power and control issues each woman has experienced.

The Power and Control Wheel

Below is the Power and Control Wheel that you discussed during the group session. Each section represents ways in which someone can be abusive to another person. Think about how this reflects your life experiences.

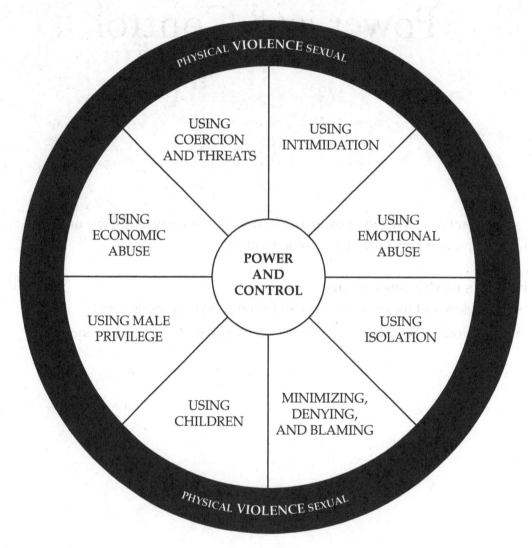

Source: Duluth Domestic Abuse Intervention Project, 202 East Superior Street, Duluth, MN 55802.

On the two pages that follow is a list of some things that can happen in relationships, based on power and control.

Beyond Anger and Violence: A Program for Women

1. **Using Intimidation**
- Making another person afraid by using looks, actions, and gestures
- Being a rageaholic
- Smashing things
- Destroying another person's property
- Abusing pets
- Displaying weapons

2. **Using Emotional Abuse**
- Putting another person down
- Making someone feel bad about herself or himself
- Calling someone names
- Telling someone that she or he is crazy
- Humiliating another person
- Trying to make someone feel guilty
- Playing mind games

3. **Using Isolation**
- Controlling what another person does, who she or he sees and talks to, what she or he reads, and where she or he goes
- Limiting another person's involvement with others
- Denying contact with family or friends
- Using jealousy to justify one's actions

4. **Minimizing, Denying, and Blaming**
- Making light of the abuse and not taking the other person's concerns about it seriously
- Saying that the abuse didn't happen
- Shifting responsibility for abusive behavior
- Saying that the other person "made you do it"

5. Using Children

- Making another parent figure feel guilty about the children
- Using the children to relay messages
- Using visitation to harass the other person
- Threatening to take away the children

6. Using Privilege

- Treating another person like a servant
- Making all the big decisions
- Acting like the "master of the castle"
- Being the one to define men's and women's roles

7. Using Economic Abuse

- Preventing the other person from getting or keeping a job
- Making a partner ask or beg you for money
- Giving another adult an allowance (like a child)
- Taking another person's money
- Not letting a partner know about or have access to family income

8. Using Coercion and Threats

- Making and/or carrying out threats to do something to hurt another person
- Threatening to leave a partner in order to get your way
- Threatening to commit suicide in order to get your way
- Threatening to report someone to the welfare or immigration authorities
- Coercing another person to drop charges
- Coercing another person to do illegal things

There also are differences in the ways that women and men use force in relationships. The table on the next page shows some of them.

Differences Between Women and Men in the Use and Effects of Force in Relationships

Method of Force	Men	Women
Intimidation	Threats and other behaviors are used to create fear in a partner, which may be followed by abuse.	Women also can create fear in others by using threats or gestures. However, they are less able to do this with men.
Isolation	Isolating a partner is an effective device used by male batterers (for example, limiting her contact with friends and family members or preventing her from working).	Women may try to limit their partners' contacts with friends, family members, or acquaintances but rarely are able to exercise control over men's behavior to the same degree that men are able to do this with women.
Economic control	In general, men are the primary wage earners and may control financial decisions.	Few women are able to successfully deny their male partners financial independence.
Sexual abuse	Men may use marital rape and sexual assault as weapons of terror.	Women may withhold sexual access and favors to manipulate their partners, but this denial does not have the same impact as a violent sexual assault.

Source: Adapted from "Just Like Men? A Critical View of Violence by Women," by S. D. Dasgupta, 1999, in M. F. Shepard & E. L. Pence (Eds.), *Coordinating Community Responses to Domestic Violence: Lessons from Duluth and Beyond*, Thousand Oaks, CA: Sage, p. 203.

Types of Abuse in Relationships

- *Use of force* is an overall term that refers to physically, verbally, and emotionally damaging behaviors used by one person toward another in order to gain short-term control of relationship dynamics. A woman may use force when trying to control or stop a partner's abusive behavior toward her.

- *Violence* is a general term that refers to any force used with the intention of causing injury.

- *Abuse* refers to isolated and random acts of violence.

- *Battering* is a systematic pattern of events that may initially seem isolated. It is a repetitive pattern of violence, the threat of violence, and/or coercively controlling behaviors or tactics, used with the intention of exerting power, inducing fear, and/or controlling another person over the long term. Coercive control is the cornerstone of battering and, therefore, battering need not include physical violence in order to be harmful. All the behaviors on the Power and Control Wheel, if repeated, create battering.

Some women who are in abusive domestic relationships describe a never-ending or continually changing pattern of abuse or violence that also fits the definition of battering.

- In the beginning, everything may seem fine. Then tension between the two people begins to build as the abuser begins to be critical, finds fault, belittles, and perhaps even threatens the woman.

- The woman tries to soothe the abusive partner by being agreeable and nurturing. Because the abuser's behavior is unpredictable, she may feel as if she is "walking on eggs."

- The abuser becomes more controlling and attempts to humiliate and isolate the woman. He or she may be angry all the time and try to blame the woman for everything. He or she may destroy the woman's property, withhold money, and threaten her. The abuser also may use drugs and/or alcohol and engage in ever more unpredictable behavior.

- The woman becomes unsure of herself and withdraws from family members and friends while trying to appease or satisfy the abuser.

- The abuser's behavior becomes more aggressive or violent. He or she may beat, rape, or imprison the woman.

- The woman attempts to protect herself, while still trying to soothe or reason with the abuser. Eventually, she may begin to fight back, may call the police, or may leave.

- Faced with the woman's action and the potential loss of the relationship, the abuser apologizes, asks for forgiveness, and promises that it will never happen again. The abuser may give the woman gifts as a token of his or her remorse. The abuser may promise to go to alcohol or drug counseling and may encourage the woman to tell her family and friends about his or her redemption.

- Convinced that the abuser is truly sorry and will change his or her attitude and behavior, the woman recommits to the relationship, cancels any legal proceedings, and may even cancel appointments with counselors because she believes that the abuser has "seen the light."

- As soon as the relationship is back where it started, the abuser begins to repeat the same behaviors: criticism, unpredictable behaviors that keep the woman uncertain and off-balance, and other forms of control and abuse. For some women, this is repeated over and over. Each time, she hopes that the abuser is really going to change.

What were your reactions to discussing abusive relationships in the group session?

The Violence Continuum

Violence in relationships can grow in intensity, or *escalate*. Often, people become angry and then react, and the situation escalates. The violence continuum in the illustration has verbal intimidation on one end of the line and homicide on the other.

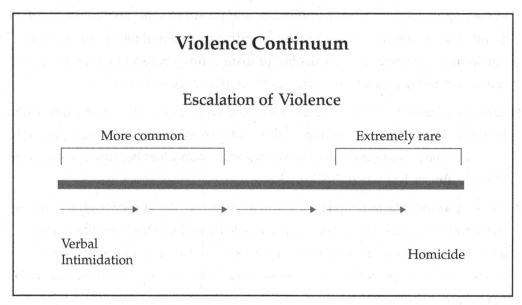

Note: Art designed by Mara Dodson, Moss Group.

On the next page are the family situations that your group discussed. Think again about how these situations might escalate into anger or violence.

Dad comes home drunk or high

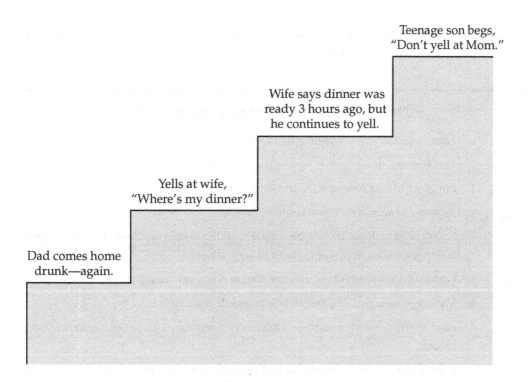

Teenage son begs,
"Don't yell at Mom."

Wife says dinner was
ready 3 hours ago, but
he continues to yell.

Yells at wife,
"Where's my dinner?"

Dad comes home
drunk—again.

Teenage girl sneaks out to meet a friend

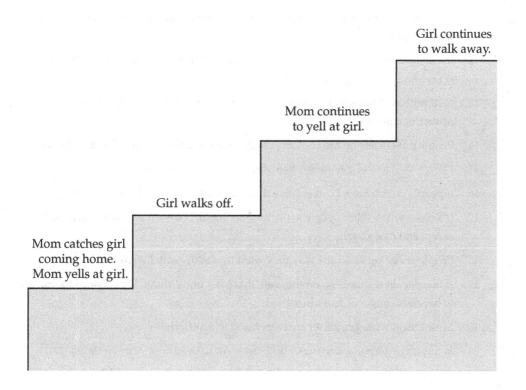

Girl continues
to walk away.

Mom continues
to yell at girl.

Girl walks off.

Mom catches girl
coming home.
Mom yells at girl.

Escalation and De-escalation

Here is the list of the statements you read aloud in the session. Which ones do you think will work best for you? You can place a check mark (√) next to those below.

De-escalating/Self-Calming Statements

_____ 1. I don't need to prove myself in this situation. I can stay calm.

_____ 2. This is no big deal.

_____ 3. I'm going to take time to relax and slow things down.

_____ 4. As long as I keep cool, I'm in control of myself.

_____ 5. I don't need to doubt myself, because what other people say doesn't matter. I'm the only person who can make me mad or keep me calm.

_____ 6. I can take a time-out if I get upset or start to notice my feeling clues.

_____ 7. My anger is a signal. It's time to talk to myself and to relax.

_____ 8. I feel angry, and that must mean I have been hurt, scared, or have some other primary feeling.

_____ 9. I can recognize that my anger comes from having my old feelings restimulated. It's okay to walk away from this fight.

_____ 10. When I get into an argument, I can take a time-out.

_____ 11. It's impossible to control other people and situations. The only thing I can control is myself and how I express my feelings.

_____ 12. It's okay to be uncertain or insecure sometimes. I don't need to be in control of everything and everybody.

_____ 13. Nothing says I have to be competent and in charge all the time. It's okay to feel unsure or confused.

_____ 14. People put erasers on the ends of pencils for a reason; it's okay to make mistakes.

_____ 15. I don't need to feel threatened here. I can relax and stay cool.

_____ 16. If people criticize me, I can survive that. Nothing says that I have to be perfect.

_____ 17. It's nice to have other people's love and approval, but even without it, I can still accept and like myself.

_____ 18. People are going to act the way they want to, not the way I want.

_____ 19. If this person wants to go off the wall, that's her or his thing. I don't need to respond to her or his anger or feel threatened.

_____ 20. Most things we argue about are stupid and insignificant.

_____ 21. Is this really important to me or do I just want to be in control or be right?

Beyond Anger and Violence: A Program for Women

You can say these statements to yourself when you notice your feeling clues escalating or when you start to feel angry. You also can come up with your own statements.

Assignment

1. First, practice the process of de-escalation. Then write about how you were able to de-escalate a touchy situation. If another person de-escalated a situation in a way that impressed you, write about that, too.

2. Next, review the Power and Control Wheel and reflect on what you have experienced in your own life. You can make some notes about that here.

3. We know that women who have experienced abuse are at risk of abusing others. The pages following the Power and Control Wheel (pages 137 and 138) contain a list of things that can happen in relationships based on power and control. When you look at the list, think about some of the things that were discussed in the session in terms of your own past and current behaviors. You may want to make some notes about these here.

4. *Optional*: You may wish to continue to fill in the Self-Reflection Tool. Although this is optional, it is highly recommended. You will find additional copies of the tool in the back of this workbook (Appendix 2).

Conflict Resolution

This session on conflict resolution focuses on a different kind of relationship: one without violence.

The goals for this session are

- To describe and practice skills for conflict resolution,
- To discuss impulsivity and the need to think before doing, and
- To examine the qualities of nonviolent relationships.

Fair Fighting

Because there is conflict in almost every type of relationship, it's important to have guidelines for how to "fight fair." The guidelines work best when both people are using them! The assumption is that a fair fight is an attempt at problem solving.

Guidelines for Fair Fighting

Fight by mutual consent.	Don't insist on a fight at a time when one of you can't handle this type of strain. A good fight demands two ready participants.
Stick to the present.	Don't dredge up past mistakes and faults about which you can do nothing.
Start with "I" statements.	When you start with "you," the other person often feels accused, and tension escalates.
Stick to the subject.	Limit this fight to this subject at hand. Don't throw every other problem into it. Consider them at a different time.
Keep it simple.	Talk about one thing at a time, not a long list of old issues.
Speak in a normal voice.	Shouting, yelling, or talking too fast can frighten or alienate or trigger the other person.
Don't hit below the belt.	In your lives together, you discover each other's sensitive areas. Don't throw them at each other.
Don't quit; work it out.	Bring the fight to a mutual conclusion. Otherwise, it will just occur again and again.
Don't try to win, EVER.	If one wins, the other loses and begins to build resentment about the relationship. That destroys rather than builds the relationship.
Respect crying.	Crying is a valid response to how we feel, but don't let crying sidetrack you. It is a response for men as well as women.

Beyond Anger and Violence: A Program for Women

Don't look away, cross your arms, or clench your fists.	This can escalate the tension.
Don't resort to violence.	Physical violence violates all of the above rules for fighting by mutual consent.

Women often ask what to do if their partners do not know the guidelines for fair fighting. The important question is, "Is your partner willing to learn them?" These guidelines work best when both people are using them. Even if your partner does not know these rules now, do you think that he or she will be willing to learn them? Willingness to learn new things is an important aspect of a relationship.

Words, Words, Words

The guidelines for fair fighting suggest that using certain words can help the situation while using other words can escalate the situation. Here are some words that escalate and words that help.

Words That Escalate	Words That Help
"You never . . ."	"I'm sorry."
"You always . . ."	"Please help me."
"I told you so."	"I made a mistake."
"I don't want to discuss it."	"Thank you."
"When will you ever learn?"	"I want to understand."
"How many times do I have to tell you?"	"I need you to . . ."
"That's a stupid thing to say."	"Can you explain that?"
"I hate it when you . . ."	"I love you."
"Where did you get that dumb idea?"	"I misunderstood . . ."

How would you feel about being in a relationship with someone who learned to use these, too?

How would you feel about being in a relationship with someone who refused to use the guidelines and tools for fair fighting?

Think about what you learned in the session on communication skills and about creating connection. Look again at the Strategies for Creating Connection in Communication on page 131 in Session Nine. With what you've learned about communication, de-escalation, and fair fighting, you may be better able to deal constructively with conflicts in your relationships.

Impulse Control

Think about a time when you acted impulsively, without thinking about the possible consequences. Maybe it was a time when you were out in the community or maybe it happened in this program. Take some time to write about this event.

If you find yourself acting impulsively, the tips that follow may help you to change this behavior.

1. Establish a daily routine. If you act impulsively with, for example, food or spending, having a routine can help you contain and manage your behavior.

2. Emotions are clues. Sometimes we express emotions impulsively. Recognize that you may have more emotional outbursts than other people. Your awareness may help you to calm yourself down. Or you can use your container to store your feelings if you feel agitated, annoyed, overwhelmed, or angry, or have any other feeling that would cause you to be impulsive.

3. If you are subject to outbursts of anger, find a pillow to punch or another safe outlet for your excess emotion. Writing about your feeling of anger also can help. Releasing the emotion safely and not directing it at others or toward yourself is much healthier and will help you release it more quickly.

4. Carry a pad of paper around with you to jot down ideas you might have during a conversation. Rather than interrupt, you can save your thoughts until there is a break. You may want to explain calmly to the person why you are writing things down.

5. If you often interrupt conversations, sit with your hand over your mouth or bite your lip softly to remind yourself to wait for a pause before speaking.

6. If you are shopping, carry only enough money for what you need. Keep credit cards and extra money locked in your car or at home. The time spent going to get your extra money will help you to consider any impulse purchase you want to make.

7. Try to recognize the difference between a *need* and a preference or want. Whether it is about buying something or about a disagreement with an important person in your life, if something is just a preference or want rather than a real need, letting it go may save you a lot of trouble in the long run.

8. Always wait to send mail (whether you are texting, e-mailing, or using snail mail) when dealing with an emotional subject. It is too easy to send things you'll regret later. Ask someone you trust to review what you wrote before sending something important.

9. Recognize that you may be impatient and have a low tolerance for frustration. When frustration is building, walk away from the situation if you can. Explain to people that you need to take time out before continuing. If you can't take a break, take a deep breath, try to relax, and focus on the aspects of the situation you can change, not on what is unchangeable.

10. Remember the time-out technique. It can be used as a way to manage impulsive behavior. A good motto is, "If in doubt, don't."

The Equality Wheel

You may be glad to learn that there are alternatives to the situations described in the Power and Control Wheel. The alternative to power and control is equality. Here is the Equality Wheel.

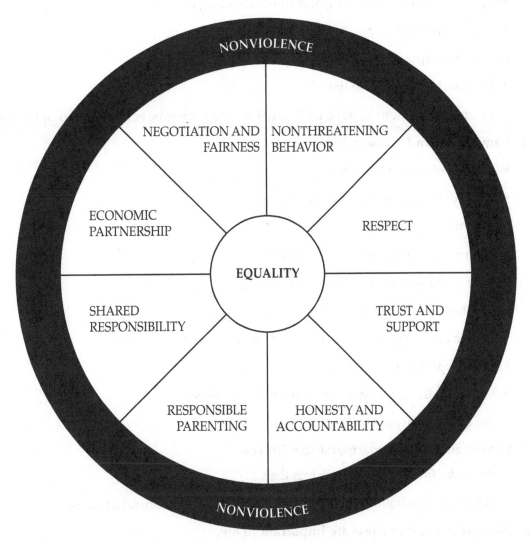

Source: Duluth Domestic Abuse Intervention Project, 202 East Superior Street, Duluth, MN 55802.

1. **I am nonthreatening.**

   - I talk and act so that you feel safe and comfortable expressing yourself and doing things.

2. **I respect you.**

   - I listen to you nonjudgmentally.

   - I am emotionally affirming and understanding of you.

   - I value your opinions.

3. **I trust and support you.**

   - I support your goals in life.

   - I respect your right to have individual feelings, friends, activities, and opinions.

4. **I am honest and accountable.**

   - I accept responsibility for myself.

   - I acknowledge my past use of violence.

   - I admit being wrong.

   - I communicate openly and truthfully.

5. **I share responsible parenting with you.**

   - We share parental responsibilities.

   - We are both positive, nonviolent role models for the children.

6. **I share responsibility with you.**

   - We mutually agree on a fair distribution of work.

   - We make family decisions together.

7. **I am in an economic partnership with you.**

   - We make financial decisions together.

   - We make sure both of us, as partners, benefit from financial agreements.

8. **Negotiation and fairness are important to me.**

   - We seek mutually satisfying solutions to conflict.

   - I accept change.

   - I am willing to compromise.

In your group discussion, you chose something to practice from the Equality Wheel. What did you choose?

Assignment

1. Use the sections of the Equality Wheel to rate, or score, yourself, first on how well you did in each area in a close relationship you once had that has now ended ("In the Past"), and then on how well you currently do in these areas in a present relationship ("Now"). The rating scale is 1 to 5, with 1 being the lowest score and 5 being the highest.

	In the Past					Now				
Trust and support	1	2	3	4	5	1	2	3	4	5
Honesty and accountability	1	2	3	4	5	1	2	3	4	5
Responsible parenting	1	2	3	4	5	1	2	3	4	5
Shared responsibility	1	2	3	4	5	1	2	3	4	5
Economic partnership	1	2	3	4	5	1	2	3	4	5
Negotiation and fairness	1	2	3	4	5	1	2	3	4	5
Nonthreatening behavior	1	2	3	4	5	1	2	3	4	5
Respect	1	2	3	4	5	1	2	3	4	5

2. Now pick one or two behaviors related to the segments to practice between now and the next session.

Creating Our Relationships

This session focuses on creating relationships; specifically, what happens when we start an intimate relationship and what we want to happen after that.

The goals of this session are
- To describe the process of falling in love,
- To compare and contrast addictive and intimate relationships, and
- To reflect on what is desired in relationships.

Falling in Love

Most people have had the experience of falling in love. This can be a wonderful experience *and* it also has the potential to create problems in our lives. This activity can help you think about love in your adult relationships.

What does it feel like to fall in love? What does it feel like to fall out of love or when a relationship ends? Write your responses and those of your group under the headings below.

Falling in Love

Falling out of Love

Beyond Anger and Violence: A Program for Women

Love and Addiction

Sometimes people become addicted to another person or addicted to the process of falling in love. These are called *addictive relationships*. What are some of the similarities between being addicted to a partner and being addicted to a drug?

Have you ever known a woman who was addicted to a person? How did she act in this relationship? Have you ever known a woman in such a relationship whose addiction to the other person made her angry at him or her?

What are the similarities between the feelings you have had when you stopped using alcohol or other drugs and your feelings when a relationship ended?

Why do you think it is useful to see this connection?

Contrasting Intimate Relationships and Addictive Relationships

Here is a description of the qualities of a healthy, intimate relationship versus those of an addictive relationship.

Intimate Relationship	Addictive Relationship
• Equality, peers.	• Power unequal (one person has more).
• Mutuality (shared, balanced).	• Imbalance.
• Choice.	• Loss of choice.
• Freedom.	• Compulsion.
• Desire to share needs and feelings.	• No-talk rule, especially if things are not working out.
• Relationship is able to include growth and change	• Relationship is always the same.
• I *want* to be there.	• I *have* to be there.
• I begin with me (self).	• I begin with you.
• I can say, "I want" and "I feel."	• You make me feel . . .
• Active, not passive.	• Reactor/responder.
• I take care of me. I am solely responsible for figuring out what I need and for communicating it to you.	• You will know what's right for me and you will fix it.
• Relationship deals with reality.	• Relationship is based on delusion/ fantasy.
• Relationship deals with things as they are, whatever comes along.	• Relationship uses denial and avoidance to deal with things.
• I have a true interest in your personal/ spiritual growth, even if it takes you away from me.	• Your spiritual growth doesn't count.
• Love is always an act of self-love.	• Love is wanting someone with me at all costs.

Source: Leaving the Enchanted Forest: The Path from Relationship Addiction to Intimacy, by S. Covington & L. Beckett, 1988, San Francisco: Harper San Francisco. Used by permission of HarperCollins.

How to End a Relationship

It is important to think about how to end relationships. Sometimes a relationship needs to end, even if you still care about or love the other person. Here is a list of things to consider when ending a relationship. You can also add to this list from your group's discussion.

- Be direct and honest.
- Be kind and sensitive.
- Avoid comments that stem from anger.
- Speak using "I" statements rather than "you" statements.
- Express feelings that you are experiencing in the present.
- Assume personal responsibility for the change.
- Decide on the level of physical and emotional intimacy you want with the person, if any.
- Act in a timely way; establish and stick to agreed-on timelines within which changes (the end of the relationship) should occur.
- Tell the person what you appreciated about the relationship and appreciated about him or her.

It is also important to think about your safety in this situation. If you are breaking up with someone you are afraid of, you will need extra support and a safety plan. Do not try to end a relationship with an abusive person when you are alone with that person.

Assignment

Answer the questions below about relationships.

1. What kind of relationships do I want to develop with others?

2. How do I want to be in these relationships?

3. Add anything else you think of to the falling-in-love and falling-out-of-love lists that you created in your group session.

Community

Our Communities

In the Orientation Session, you heard about the four layers of the social-ecological model: individual, relationship, community, and societal. This third part of the *Beyond Anger and Violence* program is about the third level of the social-ecological model: community. In these sessions, you will consider the communities that you have lived in and the places in which relationships occur, such as neighborhoods, schools, places of worship, and workplaces.

This session focuses on the characteristics or qualities of these settings that are associated with becoming a victim of violence or a victimizer (a perpetrator of violence).

The goals of this session are

- To reflect on the communities we grew up in, and
- To consider the effects of our communities on our lives.

Self-Soothing Activity: Progressive Muscle Relaxation

In Part C, you practice a progressive muscle relaxation technique, which means that you tense and then relax different muscle groups in a certain order. This is another effective strategy for calming and grounding yourself. With practice, this can help you become aware of what tension—as well as relaxation—feels like in different parts of your body. As your body relaxes, so will your mind. This is another way to develop inner peace (relaxing the mind) and outer peace (relaxing the body). You can combine deep breathing with progressive muscle relaxation for additional relief from stress.

1. Get comfortable. You may stand or sit.

2. Take a few minutes to relax, closing your eyes or lowering your eyelids, breathing in and out in slow, deep breaths.

3. When you're relaxed and ready to start, shift your attention to your right foot. Take a moment to notice the way it feels.

4. Slowly tense the muscles in your right foot, squeezing as tightly as you can. Hold for a count of ten.

5. Relax your right foot. Focus on the tension flowing away and the way your foot feels as it becomes limp and loose.

6. Stay in this relaxed state for a moment, breathing slowly and deeply.

7. When you're ready, shift your attention to your left foot. Slowly tense the muscles in your left foot as tightly as you can. Hold this for a count of ten.

8. Relax your left foot. Feel the tension flowing away as your foot relaxes. Breathe slowly and deeply.

9. Now tense the muscles in your right calf. Hold this for a count of ten.

10. Relax your right calf. Feel the tension flowing away. Breathe slowly and deeply.

11. Now tense the muscles in your left calf as tightly as you can. Hold this for a count of ten.

12. Relax your left calf. Let the tension flow away. Keep breathing.

13. Now tense the muscles in your right thigh. Hold them tight for a count of ten.

14. Relax the muscles in your right thigh. Feel the tension flow away. Breathe slowly and deeply.

15. Tense the muscles in your left thigh. Hold for a count of ten.

16. Relax your left thigh. Breathe.

17. Tense the muscles in your hips and buttocks. Hold them for a count of ten.

18. Relax your hips and buttocks. Feel the tension flowing out. Breathe.

19. Tense the muscles in your abdomen. Hold them tight for a count of ten.

20. Relax your abdomen. Feel the tension flowing out. Breathe.

21. Now tense up your chest muscles. Hold this for a count of ten.

22. Relax your chest muscles. Let the tension flow out. Breathe.

23. Now tense up your back muscles. Hold them while you count to ten.

24. Relax your back. Feel the tension flowing out. Breathe.

25. Tense the muscles in your right arm and hand. Hold them tight and count to ten.

26. Relax your right arm and hand. Let the tension flow out. Breathe.

27. Now tense up your left arm and hand. Hold for a count of ten.

28. Relax your left arm and hand and let the tension flow out. Keep breathing.

29. Tense the muscles in your neck and shoulders. Hold them tight while you count to ten.

30. Relax your neck and shoulders. Let the tension flow out of them while you breathe slowly and deeply.

31. Tense the muscles in your face. Hold for a count of ten.

32. Relax your facial muscles. Breathe slowly and deeply.

33. Now open your eyes.

This technique is especially helpful in the evening, when you are carrying around the tensions of the day.

Our Communities

Where we grow up and where we live affect our risks of being victims of violence as well as our risks of becoming people who act aggressively or violently. Your community includes the neighborhood in which you live, the schools, the places of worship, the workplaces, and the services. These all are places in which social relationships occur. Some specific risk factors for aggression and violence in communities are high unemployment, poverty, dense population or overcrowding, high residential mobility—meaning that people move around a lot and don't have stable housing— high crime levels, the existence of a local drug or gun trade, weak institutional policies (in social services, schools, workplaces, and neighborhood associations), and inadequate victim-care services. People in a community may become angry about some of these things.

In the session, you described the community you grew up in before you were eighteen. What did you realize about this community?

Visualization

The visualization activity that you did during the group session brought you back to the community or communities that you grew up in. Take a moment to quickly write about some of the things that stood out for you during this visualization. Think about the important connections in your life at that time.

Your Childhood

1. Where you lived (house, apartment, shelter, street, etc.)

2. Your room or sleeping space

3. Your family

4. Your friends

5. Your school

6. How it felt to live in your neighborhood

7. Your sense of connection to the community

8. The important or influential people in your neighborhood

9. Any gangs, drugs, or violence in your community

10. The negative influences

11. The positive influences

Your Teenage Years

1. Where you lived

2. Your high school

3. Your friends

4. Whether you felt isolated

5. How it felt to live in your neighborhood

6. Your religion, if any

7. Sports

8. Whether you drank or used drugs and/or were in a gang—or felt any pressure to do these things

9. Violence in the community

10. The negative influences

11. The positive influences

Friendship

Friends in a community are important influences. In your group, you listed the "qualities of a good friend." What were the most important ones for you?

Assignment

During the group session, you created a collage of your neighborhood or community. What was the impact of your community on your life? Write about it in the space that follows here and on the next page. While you are writing, think about

- The influence that the neighborhood had on you
- The influence that the school and/or place of worship had on you
- Who the leaders in your community were
- Who the most influential woman was
- Who the most influential man was
- Who you looked up to or wanted to be like
- Who the friends were that influenced you
- Whether there was *horizontal hostility* between girls
- Whether you ever felt betrayed or rejected by a girl who was supposed to be a friend
- Whether there was any crime
- What the common attitudes and beliefs were
- How you think all these parts of your community contributed to who you are today

You may make some drawings if you like.

What's in a Name?

Think about the qualities you bring to a friendship. Write your name down the left side of the page and add the qualities that you bring to a friendship. Use the letters in your name as the first letters for these qualities.

For example, someone named Kate might write:

Kind

Attentive

Trustworthy

Entertaining

Someone named Sue might write:

Sympathetic

Understanding

Energizing

The Importance of Safety

Safety is a very important consideration in life. In discussing families of origin and the communities you grew up in as part of previous group sessions, you will have discovered that a feeling of safety is not something that many women can take for granted.

The goals of this session are
- To discuss safety in our communities, and
- To understand the effects of our environment on our behavior.

Safety in the Community

In this session, your group discussed a sense of safety in the community. The following are the eight questions you used to guide your discussion. You may want to think more about these questions and make some notes here.

1. What did you learn about anger and/or violence in your community?

2. Did you learn anything specific about anger and/or violence from the streets?

3. How did people keep themselves safe in these communities—in their homes, schools, places of worship, stores, workplaces, and elsewhere?

4. What did you do to keep yourself safe?

5. What would need to change for your communities to be less dangerous?

6. Do you think that security guards, metal detectors, security checks, bars, locks, and alarm systems guarantee safety?

7. Do knives and guns in the community increase safety?

The Four Kinds of Safety

There are four kinds of safety. It is not enough to be physically safe; it is also important to feel safe psychologically, socially, and morally/ethically.

Use the two tables that follow as a guide as you rate safety in your life in each category. Circle the number from 1 to 5 that best fits your experience. A 1 indicates very little experience of safety, and a 5 indicates a sense of complete safety.

Four Kinds of Safety: Childhood and Teen Years

Physical safety	To be safe from physical harm	1 2 3 4 5
Psychological safety	To be able to keep one's self-discipline, self-esteem, self-control, self-awareness, and self-respect	1 2 3 4 5
Social safety	To be able to be safe with other people in relationships (to feel secure, trusted, and free to express one's thoughts and feelings) and in social settings (safe environments with connections, tolerance, and boundaries)	1 2 3 4 5
Moral/Ethical safety	To be able to maintain a set of standards, beliefs, and operating principles that are consistent, that guide behavior, and that are grounded in a respect for life	1 2 3 4 5

Source: "The Sanctuary Model," by S. Bloom. Available at http://www.sanctuaryweb.com

Four Kinds of Safety: Adult Years

Physical safety	To be safe from physical harm	1	2	3	4	5
Psychological safety	To be able to keep one's self-discipline, self-esteem, self-control, self-aware-ness, and self-respect	1	2	3	4	5
Social safety	To be able to be safe with other people in relationships (to feel secure, trusted, and free to express one's thoughts and feelings) and in social settings (safe environments with connections, toler-ance, and boundaries)	1	2	3	4	5
Moral/Ethical safety	To be able to maintain a set of stan-dards, beliefs, and operating prin-ciples that are consistent, that guide behavior, and that are grounded in a respect for life	1	2	3	4	5

Source: "The Sanctuary Model," by S. Bloom, Available at http://www.sanctuaryweb.com

You also can make some notes about how and where you may have made others feel unsafe.

Environment and Behavior

One of the things we know about human behavior is that our personalities, our past experiences, and our current environments all influence our behavior, and people act differently in different situations. The example you heard in the group session, about the Stanford Prison Experiment, showed that people's beliefs about their roles, and how they respond emotionally to that, are great influences on their behavior. The experiment showed how much the environment and circumstance can affect people and that anyone, when given complete control over others, can act abusively.

What were your thoughts and feelings after hearing about this experiment?

Safe and Unsafe Environments

In order to help to keep ourselves safe, we need to know the qualities of, and be able to tell the difference between, safe and unsafe environments. There are places where you feel safe and places where you feel unsafe. If we don't feel safe, we feel a need to protect ourselves.

Does your group in this program feel safe to you?

What makes it feel safe or not safe?

What skills are you learning in this program that you can use to create and maintain a positive community?

Safety and the Body

What do you feel physically when you think you are unsafe? What happens in your body? Where?

On page 45, under the Feelings and the Body activity, is the picture of a body that you marked earlier. Using a colored pencil or crayon, indicate where you have feelings in your body when you feel unsafe.

How do you act when you feel unsafe?

Sometimes, because of your past experiences, you can lose your ability to tell when an environment is safe or unsafe. Has this ever happened to you?

Community Maps

Below is a sample community map. When you make your map on the page that follows this one, envision the community you were in the longest as an adult or the one that had the biggest impact on you. Put yourself in the circle in the middle of the page. Then add lines connecting you to individuals in that community (represented by circles) and groups in that community (represented by squares).

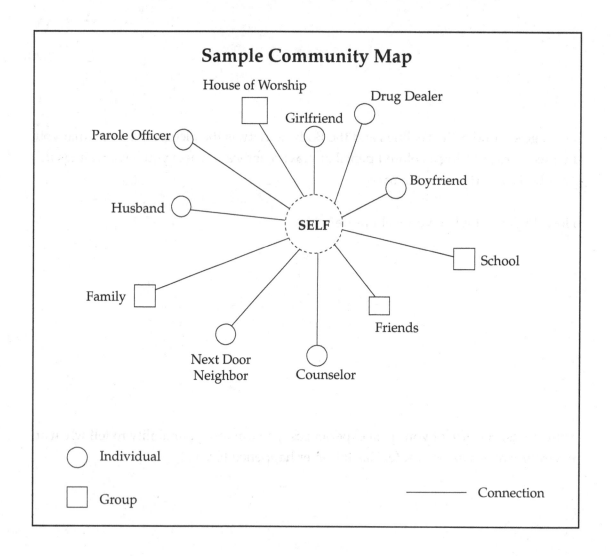

Sample Community Map

House of Worship
Drug Dealer
Girlfriend
Parole Officer
Boyfriend
Husband
SELF
School
Family
Friends
Next Door Neighbor
Counselor

○ Individual

□ Group

——— Connection

My Community Map

SELF

○ Individual

□ Group

———— Connection

What are some of the things you noticed or realized as you did your community map?

Did you find things about your community that you are angry about?

Now think about the positive changes you are making in your life, about the changes you are making because you are in this program. Before the next session, create another community map to represent your future community, your future support system. What will your new community look like? Include any support services you will use.

My Future Community Map

(SELF)

◯ Individual

▢ Group   ———— Connectior

What are some of the things you noticed or realized as you did your future community map?

Assignment

1. Take some time to finish your map of your past community. Then create a map that represents the community of support that you want in the future.

2. You also can make notes on page 180 about how and where you may have made others feel unsafe in your community.

3. Please practice the Modified Triangle yoga pose (Appendix 3).

4. Finally, you can complete the questions on page 183 about how your body feels when you are not safe.

Creating Community

This session focuses on the concept of a safe community and also on the effects of your decisions on your life.

The goals of this session are
- To view an example of a safe community, and
- To understand the short- and long-term consequences of decision making.

DVD of *What I Want My Words To Do To You*

In this session, you saw a good example of a community that women in prison have created for themselves. You may want to make notes here about the discussion you had in the group.

1. What did you see and hear that relates to the idea of community?

2. What are some of the qualities you see in the community that the women have created?

3. Eve Ensler tells the actors that there is no judgment in the writing group. How important is this?

4. Is it safe to disagree? How can you tell?

5. Do you think all the women are friends? Why or why not?

6. If they aren't all good friends, are they still positive supports for one another?

Crossroads

In the film, the women in the writing group had choices: to join the group, to participate, and to stay in the group. You have the power to make choices for yourself, too. There are many times in life when we come to a crossroad and need to make a decision or a choice. Each decision has short- and long-term consequences. A short-term consequence is the effect that a decision has right away. A long-term consequence is the effect that a decision has over a longer time period (weeks, months, even years). Sometimes people make decisions without thinking about what effects they will have in the long run. What have been some of the important crossroads in your lives? Here are some examples:

- To use or not to use alcohol, tobacco, or another drug

- To join a Twelve Step group or not to

- To use protection when having sex or not to

- To stay in or to end a particular relationship

- To use grounding exercises when stressed or triggered or not to

- To hang out or not to hang out with a person or group

- To have or not to have a fight with a friend

- To practice containment and de-escalation strategies or not to

- To seek help or not to seek help following a traumatic experience

- To engage in illegal activity or not to

- To continue to be a "people pleaser" or to become the person I want to be

What are the two or three decisions that your group focused on?

What did you notice about each decision?

What conclusions did the group members come to about how they would handle the decisions?

How do a lack of impulse control and anger affect decision making?

Making Good Decisions

Every day presents you with opportunities to chart new courses for your personal journey. The decisions you make, big or small, affect how you feel about yourself, your relationships, and your life. So it's important to make decisions and choose paths that will lead you in positive and healthy directions. Good decision making is a skill that takes effort and practice.

Here are some tips for making good decisions:

1. *Plan ahead if you can*. If you know that a tough decision is coming soon, thinking about it in advance can help you to prepare. This way, you are less likely to make an impulsive decision that you might regret.

2. *Explore your options.* There is more than one way to handle most problems. Take time to consider as many options as you can think of and weigh the pros and cons carefully.

3. *Use common sense, not just emotions*. It's easy to get carried away by your emotions and then make a decision that may not be in your best interest. It is easy to be swept away by feelings for someone or the fun of being at a party or the thrill of doing something dangerous. It is important to stop and think about the consequences of the choices that are presented to you.

4. *Ask for advice from people you trust*. People who care about you and that you respect and admire can be good sources of guidance and advice.

5. *Consider what they might do in similar situations*. Consider how someone who cares about you might react if you made a decision to do something that put you at risk. Consider how someone you admire and trust would evaluate your decision.

6. *Evaluate the results*. Once you make a decision, keep track of how that decision feels to you and the various results that it might bring. You do not need to make the same decision every time. We all make mistakes. If you make a decision that does not feel good to you, you have the power to do something different the next time.

7. *Stick by a good decision*. If you have thought through your options, sought advice from those you trust, and come to a decision that feels good to you, stick by it even if you're getting pressure from others. Trust your inner voice. Trust your instincts.

You may want to make some notes here.

Assignment

1. Identify one or two crossroads, or important decisions, that lie ahead for you. Consider how each path might affect you in the short term and how each path might affect you in the long term.

2. Write one of your choices in each of the signs on this and the next page. Describe where you think each choice might lead you in the future.

How might choosing this path affect you in the short term?

How might choosing this path affect you in the long term?

How might choosing this path affect you in the short term?

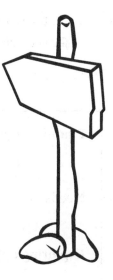

How might choosing this path affect you in the long term?

3. In the space that follows, draw a representation of the best decision that you have ever made in your life.

4. On the scale that follows, rate yourself in terms of each of the decision-making skills by circling a number.

Tips for Making Good Decisions

Planning ahead

1	2	3	4	5	6	7

Needs improvement   Good   Excellent

Exploring options (and the pros and cons of each)

1	2	3	4	5	6	7

Needs improvement   Good   Excellent

Using common sense, not just emotions

1	2	3	4	5	6	7

Needs improvement   Good   Excellent

Asking for advice from people you trust

1	2	3	4	5	6	7

Needs improvement   Good   Excellent

Evaluating the results

1	2	3	4	5	6	7

Needs improvement   Good   Excellent

Sticking by a good decision

1	2	3	4	5	6	7

Needs improvement   Good   Excellent

The Power of Community

This session completes the third part of the *Beyond Anger and Violence* program. It is the last session focused on community.

The goals of this session are
- To understand the power of community, and
- To understand the power of connection within the community.

DVD of *What I Want My Words To Do To You*

In the session, you saw the last part of the DVD. The writing group created a community. You may want to make some notes here about the discussion you had in the group.

How do you think they created a community?

What was the effect on the women in the writing group?

What made this writing group a powerful community?

What did you see on the faces of the women in the audience?

What was the effect of the writing group on the women in the audience, the larger community?

How do you think your participation in this *Beyond Anger and Violence* program and your personal growth can benefit your future community?

Activity: Writing About a Kind Act

Acts of kindness, however small, can help us to change an environment. It's these acts of kindness that help to create a safe community.

In the space below, write about an act of kindness you have seen that surprised you.

Assignment

1. Continue to work on the activity Writing About a Kind Act. You can write about any act(s) of kindness you have experienced or seen.

2. You also may want to write about your thoughts and feelings as a result of the DVD you finished watching. Using what you have learned about the power of community, you may want to answer the question, "What has been the effect of this DVD on me?" What were the three most important things for you?

PART D

Society

Society and Violence

Session Seventeen begins Part D of the *Beyond Anger and Violence* program. In this part, you focus on the society in which you live and the social and cultural ideas and behaviors that increase or decrease the risk of becoming a victim or a victimizer (perpetrator of violence).

The goals of this session are
- To examine the supports in society for violence, and
- To learn about groups that are working to stop violence.

Self-Soothing Activity: Breathing in the Positive

The breathing exercise that you will practice throughout Part D is a calming relaxation technique—another way to help you feel inner peace (quieting your thoughts and feelings) and outer peace (relaxing your body).

1. Sit in a comfortable position with your feet on the floor.

2. Breathe in, pause, then breathe out. Feel your body expand from the center and release back toward the center.

3. With each breath, breathe in a little deeper, moving the air farther into your abdomen.

4. As you breathe in, take in positive things, such as self-love, hope, courage, and joy.

5. As you breathe out, let go of the negative things that you don't want in your life, such as self-criticism, despair, stress, fear, anger, hatred, and violence.

6. Breathe in and out.

7. Do this for about a minute.

Reviewing the Risks for Violence

Here is a review of the risks for each level of violence. These risks are for being a victim of violence as well as for being a victimizer or perpetrator of violence.

Individual. A young age, a disrupted education, a lower income, substance use, and a history of abuse are factors that can increase a woman's risk of experiencing violence.

Relationship. Close friends and family members influence a woman's risk of experiencing violence. Other factors are conflict with a significant other, such as a partner or husband; male dominance; stress about money; and poor family functioning.

Community. Where a woman spends time and the people she spends it with both affect her risk. Lack of equality between males and females, lack of a stable and safe community, and a lack of resources also contribute to her risk.

Society. Risk also is affected by racist and sexist ideas and practices as well as by dislike of poor people and dislike of gay people. Lack of self-determination for women and social breakdowns following wars or disasters also put women at risk.

Certain things in society influence whether violence is encouraged or discouraged. These are things that women often feel angry about. They include

- Economic and social policies that maintain inequalities between people (such as poverty and gender inequality)
- The availability of weapons
- Socially and culturally accepted practices, such as male dominance over females, parental dominance over children, and regarding violence as an acceptable way to solve problems

The Culture Wheel

The Power and Control Wheel showed you various aspects of violence. A wheel that can help you to understand the concept of society is the Culture Wheel. The culture ring and the institutions ring show you important parts of society.

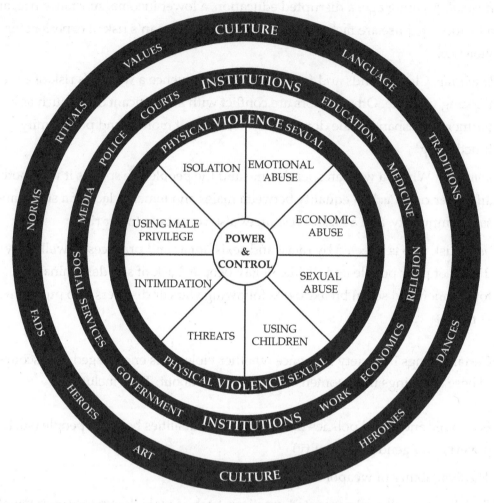

Source: Duluth Domestic Abuse Intervention Project, 202 East Superior Street, Duluth, MN 55802.

Beyond Anger and Violence: A Program for Women

Culture

- Language
- Traditions
- Heroines
- Dances
- Art
- Heroes
- Fads
- Norms
- Rituals
- Values

Institutions

- Education
- Medicine
- Religion
- Economics
- Work
- Government
- Social Services
- Media
- Police
- Courts

Institutional and Cultural Supports for Domestic Violence

In the group session, you were given some examples of the social and cultural supports for domestic violence. Fill in the chart on this page and the next one by adding examples of the tactics of power and control to the "Institutional Decisions" and "Cultural Values and Beliefs" columns.

Institutional and Cultural Supports for Domestic Violence

Tactics of Power and Control	Institutional Decisions that Support Abusers' Ability to Use Abusive Tactics	Cultural Values and Beliefs that Support Abusers
Physical abuse		
Sexual abuse		
Isolation		
Emotional abuse		

(Continued)

Beyond Anger and Violence: A Program for Women

Tactics of Power and Control	Institutional Decisions that Support Abusers' Ability to Use Abusive Tactics	Cultural Values and Beliefs that Support Abusers
Economic abuse		
Minimizing and denying		
Using children		
Threats		
Using male privilege		
Intimidation		

Source: Duluth Domestic Abuse Intervention Project, 202 East Superior Street, Duluth, MN 55802.

Working to End Violence

Here are some statistics about violence against women here in the United States and around the world:

1. Eighty-five percent of the victims of intimate partner violence are women (*Catalano, 2012*).

2. Women experience two million injuries from intimate partner violence each year (*Centers for Disease Control and Prevention, 2008*).

3. In 2010, a women experienced rape or physical violence by an intimate partner approximately every eleven seconds in the United States (*Black et al., 2011*).

4. Worldwide, an estimated one million children, mostly girls, enter the sex trade each year (*United Nations Children's Fund UK, 2004*).

5. The United States is one of the top three destinations for victims of human trafficking, along with Japan and Australia. California, New York, Texas, and Nevada are the top destinations in this country (*Coalition to Abolish Slavery and Trafficking, 2008-2009*).

6. In South Africa, a woman is killed every six hours by an intimate partner (*Krug et al., 2002*).

7. In Australia, Canada, and Israel, 40 to 70 percent of female murder victims were killed by their partners (*Krug et al., 2002*).

8. The rates of women suffering physical violence perpetrated by a current or former intimate partner range from 6 percent in China and 7 percent in Canada to over 48 percent in Zambia (*United Nations Statistics Division, 2010*).

9. Seventy percent of women in Ethiopia and Peru reported physical and/or sexual violence by an intimate partner (*World Health Organization, 2011*).

10. In the Democratic Republic of Congo, approximately 1,100 rapes are reported each month, with an average of thirty-six women and girls raped every day (*United Nations Office of the High Commissioner for Human Rights, 2010*).

11. Zimbabwe's Gender and Women's Affairs Minister reportedly stated that over 60 percent of murder cases in Zimbabwe were linked to domestic violence (*Integrated Regional Information Networks, 2007*).

12. Twenty-one percent of young women surveyed in Ghana reported that their sexual initiation was by rape (*Kristof & WuDunn, 2009*).

13. Domestic violence is the major cause of death and disability for European women aged sixteen to forty-four. It accounts for more death and ill health than cancer, road accidents, and even war (*Parliamentary Assembly of the Council of Europe, 2002*).

14. International studies reveal that approximately 20 percent of women and 5 to 10 percent of men report being victims of sexual violence as children (*World Health Organization, 2011*).

15. In a ten-country study on women's health and domestic violence conducted by the World Health Organization, between 15 percent and 71 percent of women, depending on the country, reported physical or sexual violence by a husband or partner (*World Health Organization, 2011*).

In your group session, you learned about organizations around the world that are working to stop violence against women and girls. Here is information about these organizations.

National and International Organizations

1. Amnesty International USA

Amnesty International works to stop violence against women and girls around the world who encounter rape, domestic abuse, mutilation, and other forms of gender-based violence.

2. Coalition to Abolish Slavery and Trafficking (CAST)

The Coalition to Abolish Slavery and Trafficking is dedicated to serving survivors of human trafficking and modern-day slavery (for example, sex slavery, forced domestic work, and sweatshop work). It is internationally recognized for its dedication to identifying trafficking survivors, mobilizing all sectors of a community to identify and advocate against trafficking, and providing direct services for victims.

3. National Coalition Against Domestic Violence (NCADV)

The National Coalition Against Domestic Violence works to eliminate personal and societal violence against women and children. This includes support for community-based, nonviolent alternatives, such as safe home and shelter programs for battered women and their children. It also includes public education and technical assistance, policy development and innovative legislation, and efforts to eliminate social conditions that contribute to violence against women and children.

4. National Organization for Women (NOW)

The goal of the National Organization for Women is to bring about equality for all women. It works to eliminate discrimination and harassment in the workplace, schools, the justice system, and all sectors of society; to secure abortion, birth control, and reproductive rights for all women; to end all forms of violence against women; to eradicate racism, sexism, and homophobia; and to promote equality and justice in the United States.

5. Rape, Abuse & Incest National Network (RAINN)

The Rape, Abuse & Incest National Network is the largest anti-sexual assault organization in the United States. It operates the National Sexual Assault Hotline, which offers free, confidential services.

6. V-Day: A Global Movement to End Violence Against Women and Girls

V-Day demands an end to rape, incest, battery, genital mutilation, and sexual slavery. It aims to create far-reaching awareness and lay the groundwork for new educational, protective, and legal programs throughout the world.

7. World Health Organization (WHO)

The work of the World Health Organization, a branch of the United Nations, includes the Violence Prevention Alliance—a network of international agencies and civil organizations working to prevent violence. It targets the risk factors leading to violence and promotes multi-agency cooperation. Participants are committed to implementing the recommendations of the *World Report on Violence and Health*.

Local Organizations

Your facilitator will have information about organizations in your area.

Art as an Expression of the Levels of Violence

People are working to stop violence against women in other ways. A multimedia art show called *Off the Beaten Path: Violence, Women and Art*, contains work by world-class artists to promote awareness of the root causes of violence against women, to create empathy for women's stories, to encourage conversations about how widespread the violence against women is, and to inspire the belief that women and girls can be empowered with new behavioral choices. The art exhibition focuses on five areas: the individual, the family, the community, culture, and politics. This is very similar to the focus of the social-ecological model used for this program. Here are quotations from the commentary accompanying the art show.

1. Violence and the Individual

"For the first few weeks of fertilization, boys are no different than girls. Only in the ninth week does it become clear that the sex organs will keep growing and become testicles or turn inward and develop under cover as ovaries. The female experience begins. Folding inward. Some cultures honor the mysterious unseen qualities of womanhood, but it is far more common to give power to what is seen. The girl is often expected to remain hidden, smaller, and silent."

2. Violence and the Family

"Every family begins within the body of a woman. She is the miracle maker. Her body provides the first dwelling, the first meal, the first contact. But instead of being honored as a temple, she is sometimes treated as a slave. Or worse. Women become victims of violence in their own homes more than in any other environment. There are times when a woman must break the branches of her family tree, leave the shadowy shelter, and find her own sheltering 'family' in the world."

3. Violence and the Community

"The gathering of women in solidarity leads to the development of their voices, skills, and knowledge. Free of expectations or submissiveness, surrounded by true peers, a woman can say what she needs, share what she knows, ask for credit where it is due, and learn her rights. In a true community, she rises above the noise and discovers her presence, her gravity, her wisdom. With these tools she begins to integrate into the larger community, skillfully, and with confidence."

4. Violence and Culture

"What is tradition? When should it be rejected? We live in a world in which harmful, sometimes violent, cultural practices are accepted despite the fact that they can lead to physical and psychological harm to women. It takes individual courage and group outrage to challenge deeply held and accepted belief systems. But if we are to see the world-wide problem of violence against women diminish, outrage must be channeled into peaceful action. New traditions, ones that empower rather than force people into submission, have the potential to emerge, but only if we plant seeds of understanding and compassion."

5. Violence and Politics

"A woman's role in armed conflict is rarely one of direct aggression. She is more often found acting as nurse, cook, or caregiver. But when war spirals out of the public eye, woman becomes identified as collateral, the property of man. She and her dependents are likely to lose access to adequate health care and basic living needs as greater proportions of public money are funneled into war. If she had a voice, she could be involved in the prevention of war, the attempt at resolution, the cultivation of peace. Alas, she does not."

Source: *Off the Beaten Path (Violence, Women and Art): An International Contemporary Art Exhibit*, on the website Art Works for Change, 2009. Retrieved from http://artworksforchange.org/wp-content/themes/transforms/tours/otbp_tour.htm

Assignment

1. Complete your chart of institutional and cultural supports for domestic violence.

2. Write here about your reaction to hearing about the groups that are working to stop violence.

3. Finally, look at the Equality Wheel on the next page and then assess yourself on the page after it in terms of the qualities on the wheel. After you assess yourself, you can compare your scores to the scores you gave yourself on page 155 during Part B of this program.

The Equality Wheel

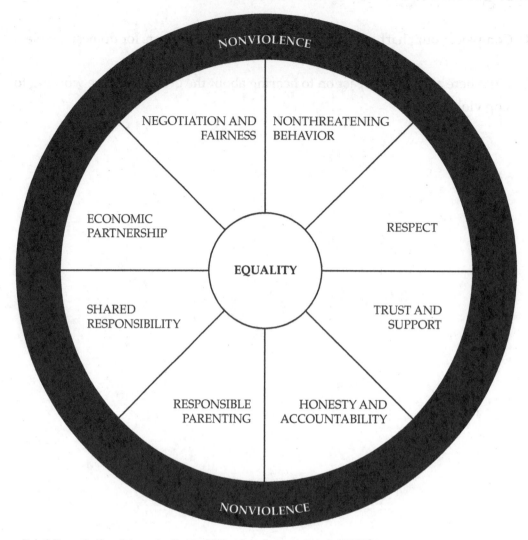

Source: Duluth Domestic Abuse Intervention Project, 202 East Superior Street, Duluth, MN 55802.

Beyond Anger and Violence: A Program for Women

Use the sections of the Equality Wheel to rate yourself on how well you are currently doing in each area. The rating scale is 1 to 5, with 1 being the lowest score and 5 being the highest score.

Trust and support	1	2	3	4	5
Honesty and accountability	1	2	3	4	5
Responsible parenting	1	2	3	4	5
Shared responsibility	1	2	3	4	5
Economic partnership	1	2	3	4	5
Negotiation and fairness	1	2	3	4	5
Nonthreatening behavior	1	2	3	4	5
Respect	1	2	3	4	5

Creating Change

This session continues the theme of society but it has a more optimistic focus. This session is about imagining a different world.

The goals of this session are

- To envision a changed society, and
- To introduce the Spirals of Transformation.

Health, Harmony, and Wholeness

In the group session, the facilitator asked you to think about these questions: What would be needed if you wanted to produce health, harmony, and wholeness in our society? What changes and decisions would you need to make personally and in your community?

The chart that you are to fill out with your group partner appears below and on the next page.

What Are the Personal, Professional, Institutional, Community, and Cultural Supports Needed for Health, Harmony, and Wholeness?			
	Decisions That Support the Conditions to be Developed		
Conditions to be Developed	**Personal and Professional**	**Institutional and Community**	**Cultural Values and Beliefs**
Physical health			
Sexual vibrancy			
Community connection			

(Continued)

Beyond Anger and Violence: A Program for Women

Conditions to be Developed	Personal and Professional	Institutional and Community	Cultural Values and Beliefs
Emotional health			
Embracing life			
Honoring children			
Feeling supported			
Equality			
Nurturance			

The Spirals of Transformation

Here is the Spiral of Violence and Nonviolence that you studied in Session One.

Spiral of Violence and Nonviolence

Transformation

Violence
(Constriction)

Nonviolence
(Expansion)

The spiral of violence is a downward spiral, and the spiral of nonviolence is an upward spiral. This image also can be used for addiction and trauma. Addiction and trauma limit our lives; they constrict us and make our personal worlds smaller.

Spiral of Addiction and Recovery

Transformation

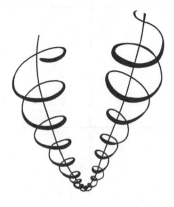

Addiction
(Constriction)

Recovery
(Expansion)

Source: Helping Women Recover: A Program for Treating Addiction, by S. Covington, 1999, San Francisco: Jossey-Bass; *Helping Women Recover: A Program for Treating Addiction* (Rev. ed.), by S. Covington, 2008, San Francisco: Jossey-Bass.

Beyond Anger and Violence: A Program for Women

Spiral of Trauma and Healing

Transformation

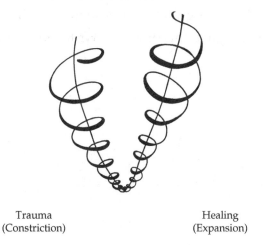

Trauma
(Constriction)

Healing
(Expansion)

Source: Beyond Trauma: A Healing Journey for Women, by S. Covington, 2003, Center City, MN: Hazelden.

There is a turning point when a woman moves from the downward spiral of addiction, and/or trauma and onto the upward spiral of recovery and healing. Growth, expansion, and wholeness are the qualities of the upward spiral. An inner transformation takes place in this process. It can occur in the shift from using anger or force to living peacefully as an individual, in a family, in a community, and in society. A woman is able to say, "Who I am today is not who I was."

Think about these spirals in terms of your own life. Where were you on the violence spiral five years ago? Where were you on the addiction spiral five years ago? Where were you on the trauma spiral five years ago? Mark these points on the spirals.

Where were you on the violence spiral six months ago? Where were you on the addiction spiral six months ago? Where were you on the trauma spiral six months ago? Mark these points too on the spirals. Where are you on these spirals today?

How have you changed?

Assignment

1. You briefly shared in your group session about what has changed positively in you since you have been in this program. Write more about this here.

2. Please practice the optional Twisted Branches to Open Wings yoga pose (Appendix 3, page 264.)

Transforming Our Lives

This session also focuses on the topics of change and transformation.

The goals of this session are
- To visualize personal transformation, and
- To discuss remorse and making amends.

Visualization

In the last session, you imagined a different world and reflected on the changes you have made since joining this program. In this session, you imagined transformation for yourself during the visualization and thought of a symbol for the positive part of it.

Write down the characteristic or behavior that you want to change and what its opposite is.

Then draw or write about your symbol and include any words or images that describe its positive qualities.

Beyond Anger and Violence: A Program for Women

The Role of Remorse in Transformation

The DVD that you have been watching shows the positive changes that the women in the writing group made in their lives, and how these women affected one another. They also had a positive effect on their own community and society inside the prison, and now they are affecting others outside the prison. When you transform your life, this transformation can affect others in your family, your community, and in your society.

One way to transform your life is through remorse, which is a feeling of guilt and regret. This is about becoming a person of integrity. Remorse is not just an apology. It means that you understand the profound effects of your behavior on another person. It's a journey of atonement—a shift from a focus on yourself to the other person. It means understanding the effects of harm you have done to others.

Here are the statements by the women in the writing group:

1. I have to remember my victim.

2. I re-live the anniversary, the date of his death.

3. I will never believe there is an explanation for what I have done.

4. What can I do to make a difference so this can't happen to anyone else?

5. I can't even enjoy anything.

6. I have to change myself to atone for his death.

These are very powerful statements from women who are changing their lives. However, several of these statements indicate that the women may be stuck in feelings of guilt and torment. Statements 4 and 6 are the ones that show deep, productive remorse.

The Process of Transformation

Here are some questions that can help you to focus on the process of change and transformation in a more personal way.

Why do I want to stop behavior that is harmful to others?

- When did I begin to make a genuine commitment to stop this harming behavior?

- What have I realized at this time?

- What opened my eyes to what I was doing?

What is important to me?

- What kinds of relationships do I want to have with people?

- What do I really want to offer or give in these relationships?

- What kinds of ways do I want to use to relate to others in these relationships?

- Where has my harmful behavior to others been leading my relationships?

- What have I been losing that is important to me?

What does it mean to be here?

- What did it take to attend these sessions? What was I up against?

- What was it like to speak out in the group?

- What was it like listening to others speak out?

- How was this different from other settings where women are together?

- What qualities do I need to find in myself?

- What qualities am I noticing in others?

Making Amends

One way to show remorse is by making amends. First, you need to decide an appropriate way to make amends to the person you have harmed. In some cases, a direct discussion may be the best approach. Sometimes this means apologizing and expressing regret for what you've done. But words are only part of making amends; you also need to make living amends by practicing new behaviors. The power of making amends is in the follow-through—the actions that back up your words.

You may have to make amends symbolically because it would hurt the people you have wronged to have contact with you or because you don't know how to find them or because they have passed away. In this case, you can do generous or helpful things instead, such as giving money or time to a charity, doing something nice for the people that the wronged ones cared about, doing something for a cause that the wronged ones cared about, or whatever lets you restore some sort of balance within yourself in honor of those you have wronged.

In the role play that you did in this session

1. How did it feel to approach another person and attempt to make amends for past behaviors?

2. What did it feel like to hear someone attempt to make amends to you?

3. What else stood out for you during this activity?

Forgiveness

Another part of harmony and transformation is forgiveness. Sometimes it is very difficult to forgive someone who has hurt you or wronged you in some way. But resentment can lead to bitterness, and those are not good things to be carrying around inside you.

How did it feel in the group session to forgive the person who has done something that you are ready to let go of?

It also is important to forgive yourself for things that you are truly sorry for doing or saying. You are not the same person that you were in the past.

How did it feel to forgive yourself?

Assignment

1. Take some time to finish answering the questions about the process of transformation that was discussed in the group (these questions are on page 230).

2. You also may want to answer the questions, "What have I done?," and, "How could I have done it?"

3. Lastly, begin to develop a forgiveness list. Make sure to include yourself.

Honoring Ourselves and Our Community

This is the last session in the *Beyond Anger and Violence* program.

The goals of this session are
- To reflect on our experiences together, and
- To say goodbye.

The Relational Wheel

The Relational Wheel represents a goal for all of us. The goal is to become relational and to develop healthy connections with one another. This is basic and essential to creating a nonviolent and more peaceful world.

   The wheel represents the experience of connection, the experience of being relational. Any time you have a meaningful connection with another person, it increases your resilience and your ability to make changes in your life.

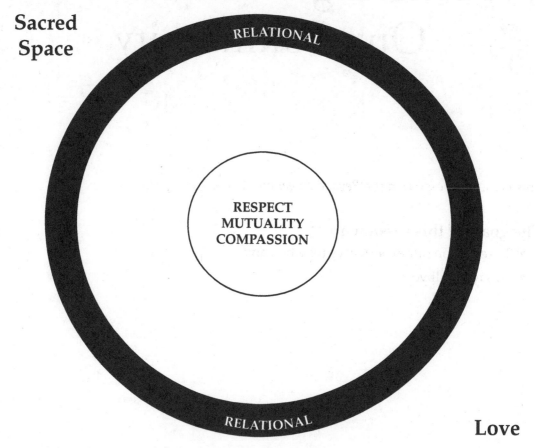

Sacred Space

RELATIONAL

**RESPECT
MUTUALITY
COMPASSION**

RELATIONAL

Love

Source: The discipline of compassion, by S. Covington and A. Dosher, 1994 (unpublished manuscript).

Power and control are at the center of violence, but respect, mutuality, and compassion are at the center of peaceful, nonviolent relationships.

- *Respect* is the appreciation of someone's values, and it begins to happen when we see that person's integrity. We often earn respect when we are willing to do the right thing, or take the right action, particularly when the choice is difficult. Respect also means seeing anew. As we begin to transform our lives, we see ourselves differently and we gain respect for ourselves.

- *Mutuality* means there is an equal investment in the relationship. Each person has the willingness and the desire to see the other as well as to be seen, to hear the other as well as to be heard, and to respect the other's vulnerability as well as to be vulnerable. Mutuality also means that there is an awareness of the "we," not just a focus on the "me."

- *Compassion* is similar to empathy, but it occurs on a deeper level. Empathy is understanding another's feelings and being able to feel them. Compassion means that we go a step further and join the person in his or her struggle or pain. When we are compassionate, we lend ourselves to another's process. We give of ourselves in order to be with the other person emotionally. It also is important that we develop compassion for ourselves.

This wheel includes sacred space and love. Love is created by respect, mutuality, and compassion. Love is a feeling but, most importantly, love is a behavior. Feeling love can be easy. Acting in a loving way often is more difficult. The challenge we all have in our lives is to become more loving human beings.

Are You Becoming the Person You Want to Be?

Please look back at page 162, in the Assignment section of Session Twelve, where you answered two questions about being in a relationship. And then look at Session Nineteen where you wrote in response to questions about the process of transformation (page 230). Now consider these additional questions as you are growing and changing.

1. How are you becoming the person you wanted to be?

2. How are you demonstrating this to yourself?

3. How are you contributing in your relationships?

4. What are you offering others?

5. How are you showing love, respect, and compassion?

6. Are you also giving these to yourself?

ORID

You used a specific process of decision making in this session to help yourself think about your group over the past few months. You can use this four-step process to help you make many of your future decisions.

OBJECTIVE (What Is?)

The first stage of the process is *Objective*. This means getting the facts through observation and remembering information and details that re-create the experience. In the group session, you thought back over the past twenty sessions in this program and then answered the questions: "What have you seen?," and, "What have you heard?"

REFLECTIVE (Looking Within)

The second stage is *Reflective*. This is when we reflect on our emotional reactions to the event or experience. When you thought about your experiences in the *Beyond Anger and Violence* program, what were some of your typical feelings? What were the high points for you? What were the low points?

INTERPRETIVE (What Is the Meaning?)

The third stage is *Interpretive*. This is when we consider the meaning and impact of the experience, its significance or usefulness, and its value. What was your greatest learning or insight from the group sessions? What is the meaning or significance of these sessions for you? What has been important for you?

DECISIVE (What Should I Do?)

The last stage is *Decisive*. Given what you have seen, heard, and felt—and what these meant to you—what decisions do you need to make based on what you have learned? What decisions will you make, and what actions will you take to put these decisions into practice?

    This is called the ORID process. You can use it to think about any occurrence or event. It is a tool for looking at your experiences and making good decisions by finding your own truths.

Appreciation

It is time to appreciate all that you have done to create a safe group that has served as a passage for you on your journey to wholeness and transformation. You and each woman in the group are now part of a larger circle of women working for a nonviolent world. This is not an end; it is a new beginning.

"We must become the change we want to see."

— Author Unknown

This flower is a lotus. It is a symbol of transformation.

APPENDIX I DAILY ANGER LOG

Daily Anger Log

Day of Week	What Happened (add any smoking, overeating, and use of alcohol or other drugs)	Intensity of My Anger 1 = Irritated 2 = Mildly angry 3 = Very angry 4 = Furious/enraged	Amount of Time I Felt Angry
Sunday			
Monday			
Tuesday			
Wednesday			
Thursday			
Friday			
Saturday			

Daily Anger Log

Day of Week	What Happened (add any smoking, overeating, and use of alcohol or other drugs)	Intensity of My Anger 1 = Irritated 2 = Mildly angry 3 = Very angry 4 = Furious/enraged	Amount of Time I Felt Angry
Sunday			
Monday			
Tuesday			
Wednesday			
Thursday			
Friday			
Saturday			

Beyond Anger and Violence: A Program for Women

Daily Anger Log

Day of Week	What Happened (add any smoking, overeating, and use of alcohol or other drugs)	Intensity of My Anger 1 = Irritated 2 = Mildly angry 3 = Very angry 4 = Furious/enraged	Amount of Time I Felt Angry
Sunday			
Monday			
Tuesday			
Wednesday			
Thursday			
Friday			
Saturday			

Daily Anger Log

Day of Week	What Happened (add any smoking, overeating, and use of alcohol or other drugs)	Intensity of My Anger 1 = Irritated 2 = Mildly angry 3 = Very angry 4 = Furious/enraged	Amount of Time I Felt Angry
Sunday			
Monday			
Tuesday			
Wednesday			
Thursday			
Friday			
Saturday			

Beyond Anger and Violence: A Program for Women

Daily Anger Log

Day of Week	What Happened (add any smoking, overeating, and use of alcohol or other drugs)	Intensity of My Anger 1 = Irritated 2 = Mildly angry 3 = Very angry 4 = Furious/enraged	Amount of Time I Felt Angry
Sunday			
Monday			
Tuesday			
Wednesday			
Thursday			
Friday			
Saturday			

Daily Anger Log

Day of Week	What Happened (add any smoking, overeating, and use of alcohol or other drugs)	Intensity of My Anger 1 = Irritated 2 = Mildly angry 3 = Very angry 4 = Furious/enraged	Amount of Time I Felt Angry
Sunday			
Monday			
Tuesday			
Wednesday			
Thursday			
Friday			
Saturday			

Beyond Anger and Violence: A Program for Women

Daily Anger Log

Day of Week	What Happened (add any smoking, overeating, and use of alcohol or other drugs)	Intensity of My Anger 1 = Irritated 2 = Mildly angry 3 = Very angry 4 = Furious/enraged	Amount of Time I Felt Angry
Sunday			
Monday			
Tuesday			
Wednesday			
Thursday			
Friday			
Saturday			

Daily Anger Log

Day of Week	What Happened (add any smoking, overeating, and use of alcohol or other drugs)	Intensity of My Anger 1 = Irritated 2 = Mildly angry 3 = Very angry 4 = Furious/enraged	Amount of Time I Felt Angry
Sunday			
Monday			
Tuesday			
Wednesday			
Thursday			
Friday			
Saturday			

Beyond Anger and Violence: A Program for Women

Self Reflection Tool

Date							
AM							
PM							

Date							
AM							
PM							

If I am below 5, I will share with _____ or _____ or _____.

[1]To review the instructions, see Session Six, pages 95, 96, and 98.

251

Self Reflection Tool

Date							
AM							
PM							

Date							
AM							
PM							

If I am below 5, I will share with _____ or _____ or _____.

Beyond Anger and Violence: A Program for Women

Self Reflection Tool

Date						
AM						
PM						

Date						
AM						
PM						

If I am below 5, I will share with _____ or _____ or _____ .

Self Reflection Tool

Date							
AM							
PM							

Date							
AM							
PM							

If I am below 5, I will share with _____ or _____ or _____.

Self Reflection Tool

Date							
AM							
PM							

Date							
AM							
PM							

If I am below 5, I will share with _____ or _____ or _____.

Self Reflection Tool

Date							
AM							
PM							

Date							
AM							
PM							

If I am below 5, I will share with _____ or _____ or _____.

256

256

Beyond Anger and Violence: A Program for Women

Self Reflection Tool

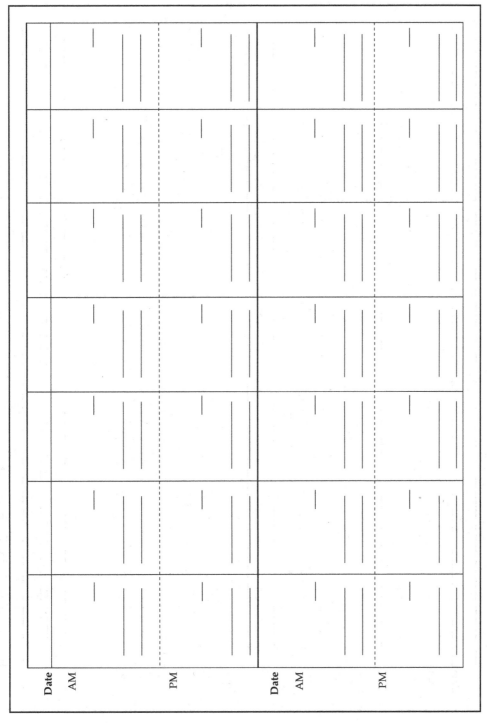

Date							
AM							
PM							
Date							
AM							
PM							

If I am below 5, I will share with _____ or _____ or _____.

Self Reflection Tool

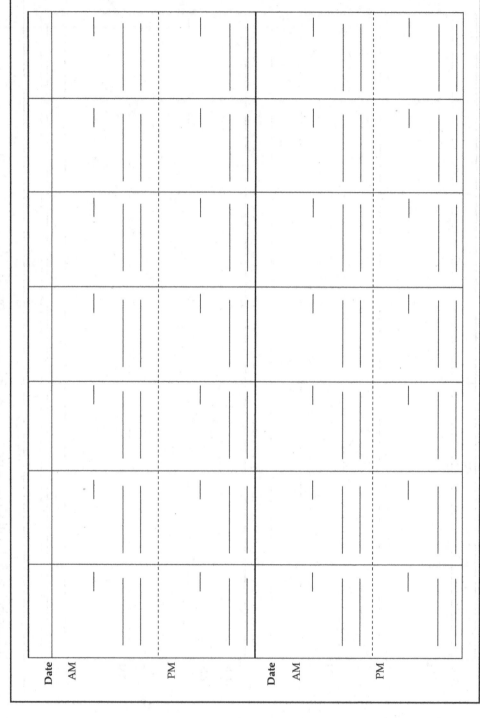

Date							
AM							
PM							
Date							
AM							
PM							

If I am below 5, I will share with _____ or _____ or _____.

Self Reflection Tool

Date							
AM							
PM							

Date							
AM							
PM							

If I am below 5, I will share with _____ or _____ or _____ .

Self Reflection Tool

Date
AM
PM

Date
AM
PM

If I am below 5, I will share with _____ or _____ or _____.

1. Breath of Joy

Purpose: The Breath of Joy exercise connects the use of breath with body movements to aid a physical and emotional release of tension. The person then feels relaxed yet energized. This exercise is beneficial for letting go (or at least loosening the grip) of long-held anger or grief that has been stored in the physical body or in habitual thought patterns that no longer are supportive for growth. This physical and emotional release assists people to become willing to adopt new ideas, thought patterns, and behaviors for personal development. The Breath of Joy consists of three quick and consecutive inhalations through the nose and one audible exhalation through the mouth. These breaths are synchronized with arm movements to engage the whole body.

| Inhale forward | Inhale sideways | Inhale overhead | Exhale while swinging arms |

[1]The yoga poses described (and accompanying photos) are recommended by Machelle Lee, a certified and registered yoga instructor and massage therapist. Machelle has a master's degree in mythology and depth psychology. Since 1991, she has led therapeutic-movement and yoga classes in various parts of the United States. Machelle weaves together modern psychology and different styles of yoga in a creative and grounded approach to self-development. She can be reached at www.machellelee.com.

Practice: Begin in a standing position with the feet about hip-width apart. Take a short inhalation through the nose while bringing the arms straight out in front of the chest. Take another quick inhalation through the nose while opening the arms wide in a "T" shape. Take one last inhalation while reaching the arms straight overhead. With an audible "ahh" sound, exhale through the mouth while bringing the arms in a sweeping motion down to the side of the body.

Once the pattern of synchronizing the breath with movement is comfortable, create a fuller body expression by bending the knees while dropping the chest into a forward bend during the exhalation and letting the arms swing down and past the hips.

Repeat by rising to a standing position and inhaling through the nose with the arms forward. Inhale a bit more while spreading the arms out into the "T" position. Inhale to the fullest lung capacity while bringing the arms overhead. Finally, bend forward with the knees bent, exhaling through the mouth as the arms swing down and past the hips.

Repeat 5 to 10 times in a rhythmic flow.

For those who have limited mobility, a modification is to come down only halfway on the exhale.

2. Seated Pigeon's Pose

Purpose: The Seated Pigeon's Pose provides a deep stretch through the side of the hip and the band of tissues that connects the outer hip and the outer side of the knee. This band of tissues often is tight, which can cause lower back pain, knee challenges, and aggravation of the sciatic nerve—sometimes felt as "shooting" pain through the outer hip, leg, or groin. Giving these tissues a modest stretch with this pose can bring a relief from aches and also increase physical comfort when sitting or walking. Practicing this pose also can provide an emotional release of stress or trauma around the hips. It can aid in the release of anger or depression. Some people experience a physical feeling of release or relief, and others exhibit an emotional response, such as tears.

Practice: Begin while seated in a chair with both feet on the ground. Place the left foot on the right knee, so that the legs resemble a number "4" when looking down at the shape. Some people feel a tug immediately on the side of the left hip or buttock. It may radiate down the side of the leg toward the knee. If it is not felt in these areas, simply lean forward. As the torso moves forward toward the legs, the tension to the outer hip is increased. You can hold onto the seat of the chair for support or lean your forearms on your knees. Hold the pose for 1 to 3 minutes for optimal results. Then repeat with the leg positions reversed. Breath deeply while holding the pose.

3. Modified Triangle

Purpose: The Modified Triangle exercise targets tissues in the inner legs, lower back, and hips. It offers a nice stretch to the side of the body and ribs. The spinal twist massages and supports the spinal column and soothes the nerves that branch out from each of the vertebrae and connect with every other part of the body. Symbolically, the triangle, or pyramid shape, represents the balance and unity among the three interconnected aspects of being: mind, body, and spirit.

Practice: Stand in front of the seat of a chair. Hold the arms out to the sides in a "T" position and then open the legs wide until the ankles are under the wrists. The wide stance offers a solid and steady foundation to the pose. Place both hands on the seat of the chair (about the width of the shoulders), keeping the arms straight. Bend forward from the hips. This may yield a nice hamstring stretch and can be held for several breaths.

To continue into the Modified Triangle pose, with the legs straight, keep the left foot facing forward but pivot the right foot out so its toes point to the side. This will create a tug to the inner right leg. Next, reach toward the ceiling or sky with the left arm and hand. The left hip will follow so that your chest and gaze will be toward the left. Hold the pose for 5 to 10 breaths. This exercise stretches the inner leg while rotating the spine in a gentle twist, stimulating the tissues of the lower back.

If you have difficulty reaching upward with a straight arm, you can place your reaching hand on your hip instead and enjoy the twist of the spine.

Bring both hands back to the seat and repeat the exercise on the other side (the right foot points forward as the left foot pivots to the side and the right hand reaches upward).

4. Twisted Branches to Open Wings

Purpose: The Twisted Branches and Open Wings poses complement one another and offer muscular release to the upper back, shoulders, and chest. When practiced together, they work in harmony to stimulate the lungs and heart. Lungs symbolically represent the ability to let go of stagnant energy (exhaling) and invite in new life and possibility (inhaling). Combining breath and movement aids the transformation of grief into a desire to explore the fullness of life and to feel safe doing so. Stimulating the heart serves the transition out of anxiety and into the ability to trust one's intuition and insight, create healthy boundaries, and experience joy.

Practice: Because each person's bone structure is different, Twisted Branches can be performed in a number of ways so that you can find the one that feels best for your body. The gentlest pose is simply to cross the arms in front of the chest, resting the crossed hands on the shoulders in what looks like a self-hug. Do this while taking 5 to 10 breaths.

The second option is to cross the upper arms by resting the elbow of one arm in the soft elbow crease of the opposite arm. The hands may be back to back, or you may be able to bring the palms together. Crossing the arms in front causes the shoulder blades to stretch, which facilitates the release of tension in the upper back. Take 5 to 10 breaths.

Then release the arms and clasp the hands together behind the back to create the Open Wings pose. Depending on your bone structure and level of comfort, the arms can be straight or the elbows can be bent. This compresses and relaxes the tissues of the upper back and the shoulder blades, while simultaneously offering a stretch across the chest.

Drop the chin toward the chest to provide a new level of release in the back of the head, neck, and upper back. Hold the pose while taking 5 to 10 breaths.

Repeat the Twisted Branches with the other arm on top and then complete another Open Wings pose.

REFERENCES

Art Works for Change. (2009). *Off the beaten path (Violence, women and art): An international contemporary art exhibit*. Retrieved from http://artworksforchange.org/wp-content/themes/transforms/tours/otbp_tour.htm

Black, M. C., Basile, K. C., Breiding, M. J., Smith, S. G., Walters, M. L., Merrick, M. T., . . . & Stevens, M. R. (2011). *The national intimate partner and sexual violence survey: 2010 summary report*. Atlanta, GA: National Center for Injury Prevention and Control, Centers for Disease Control and Prevention. Retrieved from http://www.cdc.gov/violenceprevention/pdf/nisvs_report2010-a.pdf

Catalano, S. (2012). *Intimate partner violence, 1993–2010*. Washington, DC: U.S. Department of Justice, Office of Justice Programs, Bureau of Justice Statistics. Retrieved from http://www.bjs.gov/content/pub/pdf/ipv9310.pdf

Center for Communication and Social Policy, University of California, Santa Barbara. (1998). Executive summary, in National television violence study, Vol. 3. Thousand Oaks, CA: Sage.

Centers for Disease Control and Prevention. (2008, February). Adverse health conditions and health risk behaviors associated with intimate partner violence—United States, 2005. *Morbidity and Mortality Weekly Report, 57*(5), 113–117. Retrieved from http://www.cdc.gov/mmwr/preview/mmwrhtml/mm5705a1.htm

Children's Defense Fund Ohio. (2009, October). *Children who witness domestic violence* (Kids Count Issue Brief). Retrieved from http://www.cdfohio.org/research-library/documents/resources/children-who-witness-domestic-violence-ohio.pdf

Coalition to Abolish Slavery and Trafficking. (2008–2009). *Key stats: A serious problem—around the globe and in the USA*. Retrieved from http://www.castla.org/key-stats

Covington, S. (2003). A woman's journey home: Challenges for the female offender. In J. Travis & M. Waul (Eds.), *Prisoners once removed*. Washington, DC: The Urban Institute.

Covington, S. (2007). The relational theory of women's psychological development: Implications for the criminal justice system. In R. T. Zaplin (Ed.), *Female offenders: Critical perspectives and effective interventions* (2nd ed., pp. 135–164). Sudbury, MA: Jones & Bartlett.

Covington, S., & Surrey, J. (2000). *The relational theory of women's psychological development: Implications for substance abuse* (Stone Center Work in Progress no. 91). Wellesley, MA: Stone Center Working Papers Series.

Dahlberg, L. L., & Krug, E. G. (2002). Violence: A global health problem. In E. Krug, L. L. Dahlberg, J. A. Mercy, A. B. Zwi, & R. Lorenzo (Eds.), *World report on violence and health* (pp. 1–56). Geneva: World Health Organization.

Duran, E., Firehammer, J., & Gonzalez, J. (2008, Summer). Liberation psychology as the path toward healing cultural soul wounds. *Journal of Counseling and Development, 86*, 288–295.

Every Child Matters Education Fund. (2008). *We can do better: Child abuse and neglect deaths in America*. Washington, DC: Author.

Family Violence Prevention Fund. (2009). *Children and domestic violence, 2008*. San Francisco: Author.

Federal Bureau of Investigation. (2008). *Crime in the United States*. Washington, DC: U.S. Department of Justice.

Felitti, V., & Anda, R. (2010). The relationship of adverse childhood experiences to adult medical disease, psychiatric disorders and sexual behavior: Implications for healthcare. In R. Lanius & E. Vermetten (Eds.), *The hidden epidemic: The impact of early childhood trauma on health and disease* (pp. 77–87). Cambridge, England: Cambridge University Press.

Integrated Regional Information Networks. (2007, January 10). Zimbabwe: New law set to bring hope to abused women. Retrieved from http://www.irinnews.org/PrintReport.aspx?ReportId=64384

Kristof, N., & WuDunn, S. (2009, September 23). The women's crusade. *The New York Times Sunday Magazine*.

Krug, E. G., Dahlberg, L. L., Mercy, J. A., Zwi, A. B., & Lozano, R. (2002). *World report on violence and health*. Geneva: World Health Organization.

Messina, N., & Grella, C. (2006). Childhood trauma and women's health outcomes: A California prison population. *The American Journal of Public Health, 96*(10), 1842–1848.

Napoli, M. (2006). *Tools for balanced living: A mindfulness practice workbook* (2nd ed.). Scottsdale, AZ: Performance Dimensions.

National Association of State Mental Health Program Directors. (2008). *Training curriculum for the reduction of seclusion and restraint*. Alexandria, VA: National Technical Assistance Center, Author.

National Center for Missing and Exploited Children. (2008). *Every child deserves a safe childhood: 2008 annual report*. Alexandria, VA: Author.

National Organization for Women. (2009). *Violence against women in the United States: Statistics*. Washington, DC: Author. Retrieved from http://www.now.org/issues/violence/stats.html

Office of Juvenile Justice and Delinquency Prevention. (2008). *Charting the way to delinquency prevention for girls* (Girls Study Group). Washington, DC: U.S. Department of Justice.

Parliamentary Assembly of the Council of Europe. (2002). *Recommendation 1582 (2002): Domestic violence against women*. (Adopted September 27, 2002.) Retrieved from http://assembly.coe.int/Documents/AdoptedText/TA02/EREC1582.htm

Pollock, J., Mullings, J., & Crouch, B. (2006). Violent women: Findings from the Texas Women Inmates Study. *Journal of Interpersonal Violence, 21*(4), 485–502.

Taylor, L. R., & Gaskin-Laniyan, N. (2007, January). Sexual assault in abusive relationships. *NIJ Journal, 256* (NCJ 216525). Retrieved from http://www.nij.gov/journals/256/sexual-assault.html

United Nations Children's Fund UK. (2004, January 28). *Commercial sexual exploitation position statement*. Retrieved from http://www.unicef.org.uk/campaigns/publications/pdf/sexual_exploitation06.pdf

United Nations Office of the High Commissioner for Human Rights. (2010). *Report of the mapping exercise documenting the most serious violations of human rights and international humanitarian law committed within the territory of the Democratic Republic of the Congo between March 1993 and June 2003*. Retrieved from http://www.unhcr.org/refworld/docid/4ca99bc22.html

United Nations Statistics Division (2010). *The world's women 2010: Trends and statistics* (United Nations Publications ST/ESA/STAT/SER.K/19). New York: Author, p. 131.

Walley-Jean, J. C. (2009). Debunking the myth of the "angry black woman": An exploration of anger in young African American women. *Black Women, Gender & Families, 3*(2), 68–86.

Whitfield, C. L., Anda R. F., Dube, S. R., & Felitti, V. J. (2003). Violent childhood experiences and the risk of intimate partner violence in adults: Assessment in a large health maintenance organization. *Journal of Interpersonal Violence, 18*(2), 166–185.

Wight, V. R., Chau, M., & Aratani, Y. (2010). *Who are America's poor children? The official story*. New York: National Center for Children in Poverty, Mailman School of Public Health, Columbia University. Retrieved from http://www.nccp.org/publications/pdf/text_912.pdf

Wilson, B. (2002). Violence in children's television programming: Assessing the risks. *Journal of Communication, 52*, 5–35.

Women's Law Project. (2002, September). *Responding to the needs of pregnant and parenting women with substance use disorders in Philadelphia*. Philadelphia, PA: Author. Retrieved from http://www.womenslawproject.org/resources/Pregnant_parenting_PVS.pdf

World Health Organization. (2004). *Preventing violence: A guide to implementing the recommendations of the World Report on Violence and Health*. Geneva: Author.

World Health Organization. (2011, September). *Violence against women fact sheet*. Retrieved from http://www.who.int/mediacentre/factsheets/fs239/en/index.html

ABOUT THE AUTHOR

Stephanie S. Covington, PhD, LCSW, is a nationally recognized clinician, author, and organizational consultant noted for her pioneering work on women's issues. For over twenty-five years her work has focused on the creation of progressive, innovative, gender-responsive, and trauma-informed services. Her extensive experience includes designing women's services at the Betty Ford Center, developing programs for women in criminal justice settings, and being the featured therapist on the Oprah Winfrey Network television show *Breaking Down the Bars*. Dr. Covington also has served as a consultant to the United Nations Office on Drugs and Crime (UNODC) in Vienna and was selected for the Federal Advisory Council on Women's Services. She has trained social service professionals in the United States, Mexico, Europe, Africa, and New Zealand and has published extensively, including eight gender-responsive, trauma-informed treatment curricula and three best-selling self-help books. Dr. Covington is based in La Jolla, California, where she is co-director of both the Institute for Relational Development and the Center for Gender and Justice.

ABOUT THE COVER

I chose a lotus flower for the cover of *Beyond Anger and Violence* because the lotus can be a meaningful symbol of a woman's transformation. Although it grows with its roots deep in the mud, the lotus rises from the muddy waters and emerges pure and unblemished. It unfolds gradually, one petal at a time, to blossom in the sunlight.

The mud can symbolize murky beginnings or the dark side of anger as well as the experience of trauma and/or addiction. The water can symbolize a developmental experience or a transition to healing and recovery. The lotus can symbolize the purity of the soul, rebirth, spiritual awakening, and enlightenment. For thousands of years, the lotus has been associated with profound change.

I see the lotus as the symbol of a woman's healing and recovery. Making the shift from anger, aggression, or violence to calmness, nonviolence, and peace is a transformational experience. When a woman makes this shift, she is able to say, "Who I am today is not who I was." The elegant and beautiful lotus flower that emerges from the mud is the beautiful woman within.

FEEDBACK FORM

Beyond Anger & Violence:
A Program for Women

Dear Participant:

I would appreciate hearing about your experience with the *Beyond Anger & Violence* program. Any information you would like to share with me will be greatly appreciated.

Describe yourself:

Describe where you participated in this program:

Your experience with *Beyond Anger & Violence* program:

What did you find most useful?

Why? How?

What did you find least useful?

Why? How?

Other suggestions or comments:

Thank you for your input.

Please return this form to:

Stephanie S. Covington, Ph.D.
Institute for Relational Development
Center for Gender and Justice
7946 Ivanhoe Avenue, Suite 201B
La Jolla, CA 92037
Fax: (858) 454-8598
E-mail: sc@stephaniecovington.com
www.stephaniecovington.com